I Love

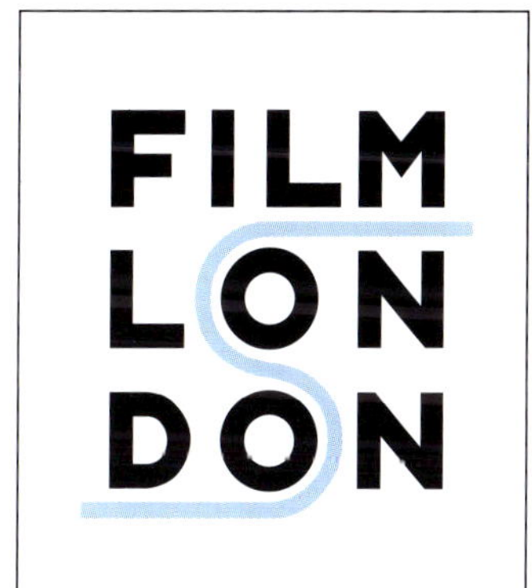

ON LOCATION

Photography by Jamie Lumley
Produced by Film London

Published in Great Britain by Film London,
Suite 6.10, The Tea Building,
56 Shoreditch High Street, London E1 6JJ

ISBN 0-9553972-0-0
ISBN 978-0-9553972-0-2

A catalogue record for this book is available from the British Library.

Editor: Film London
Chief Executive: Adrian Wootton
Project Staff: Alison Williams, Sophie Goldspink and Daniela Kirchner
Photography: Jamie Lumley
Layout: Matt @ Free Thinking Design
Printed and bound by: Print Solutions Partnership, England

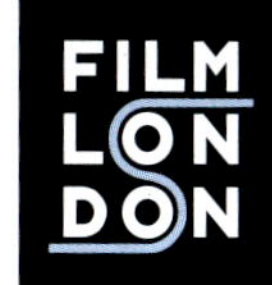

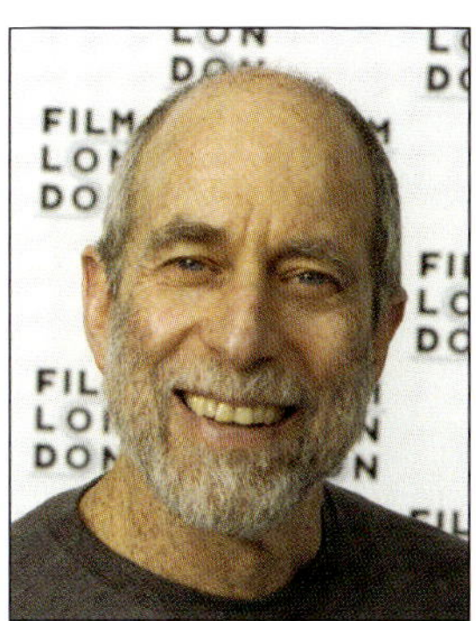

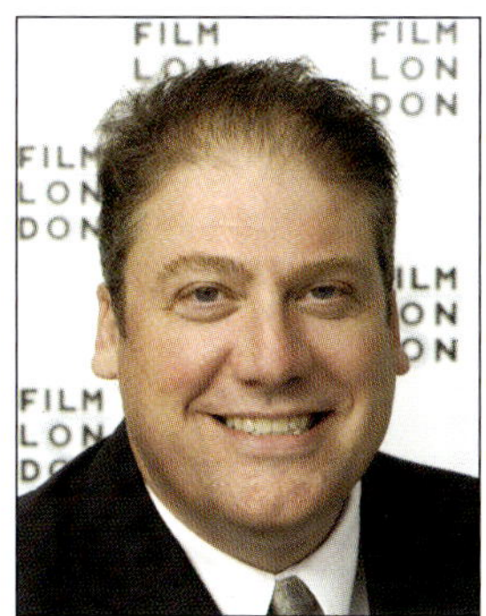

London is a city of many histories: political, social and aesthetic. Aside from its architecture, London has perhaps, and somewhat perversely, been most projected through the written word. It is the theatrical home of Shakespeare, of Grub Street, of Dr Johnson, the space of the scribe, of the grand novelist, especially of Dickens. Yet, in the 20th Century, London logically became the home, the centre and the fulcrum of the British film industry.

The visual poetry rendered in the film studio and, post World War II, in the street, began to represent the city, its culture and its history. As London changed, so did cinema's depiction of it, from Alfred Hitchcock in the 30s; David Lean in the 40s; through Lewis Gilbert's *Alfie* in the 60s; to the Working Title blockbusters, like *Four Weddings and a Funeral*. Also, and strangely, London disguises itself, it counterfeits for imagined places - Batman's Gotham City; Charlie's Chocolate Factory.

With so much filmed and filming, it is amazing that it is only recently that London has been recognised as this flexible, diverse, plastic place which can reflect itself and so many other cities, climates and cultures. In other words, it is only now that London's place as a major film-making centre is recognised and it can be appreciated that it is extremely attractive to many of the world's greatest film-makers. A fact which is reflected in the entries in this book.

This recognition brings a new challenge: with greater awareness there is hopefully greater demand, and hopefully greater demand means more architecture, more cityscape will be available for cinema to utilise. Thankfully, there is so much in this city which is not clichéd or over determined, that we have the chance to proffer film-makers constantly evolving new backdrops, enriching and enlarging the visual lexicon of film-makers who come to make movies here. Our belief is to release film-makers' imagination, not circumscribe it and London's greatness as a city is that evolution and diversity allows us to represent, newly discover and reveal the wonders of what we believe is the greatest city on earth.

Sandy Lieberson
Chair, Film London

Adrian Wootton
Chief Executive, Film London

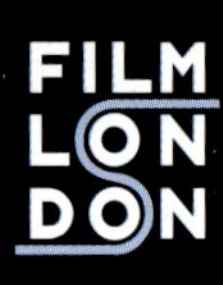

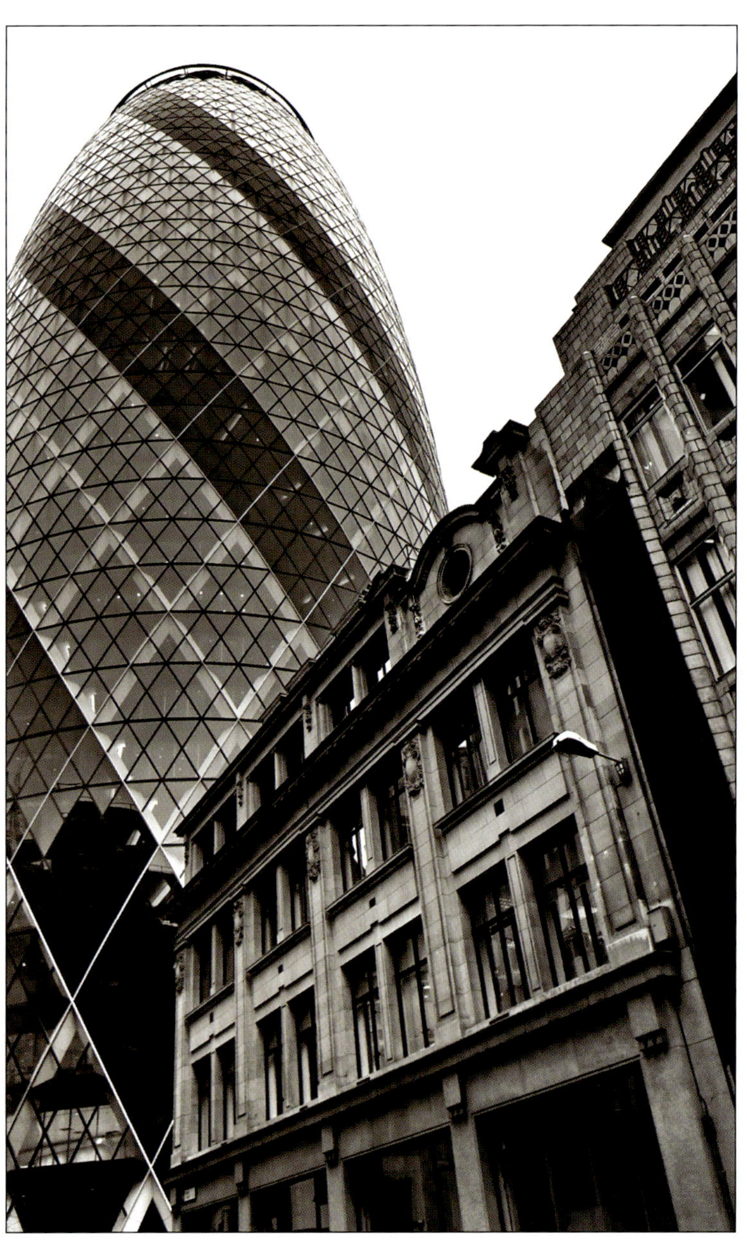

I've spent quite a lot of my life working in some of the most beautiful cities and exotic locations in the world, with actors from all over the world, and I always find it surprising when they say 'Oh I love London. London is so beautiful. You're so lucky to live in London. It's great to work in London.' At the time I always think they're going over the top. But then I come home and there She is. Every time I come back from a long job, I'm always gobsmacked by how beautiful London really is. We live here all the time, all running about with our heads down, busy, busy, busy. We never look up. We don't see Her anymore. We just take Her for granted. But just stop and take a really good look at this town. None of those actors were going over the top. London is beautiful. And we are incredibly lucky to live here. And working here, I'm telling you, it's the best. I've been asked countless times. 'When are you going to move to LA, Bob? You'd have the weather, you could make Hollywood movies. You could live like a real film star.' And I always think, 'Naaaa, I'm a Londoner'. 'Nough said.

Bob Hoskins

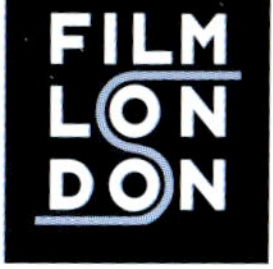

View towards Seven Dials from the Palace Theatre

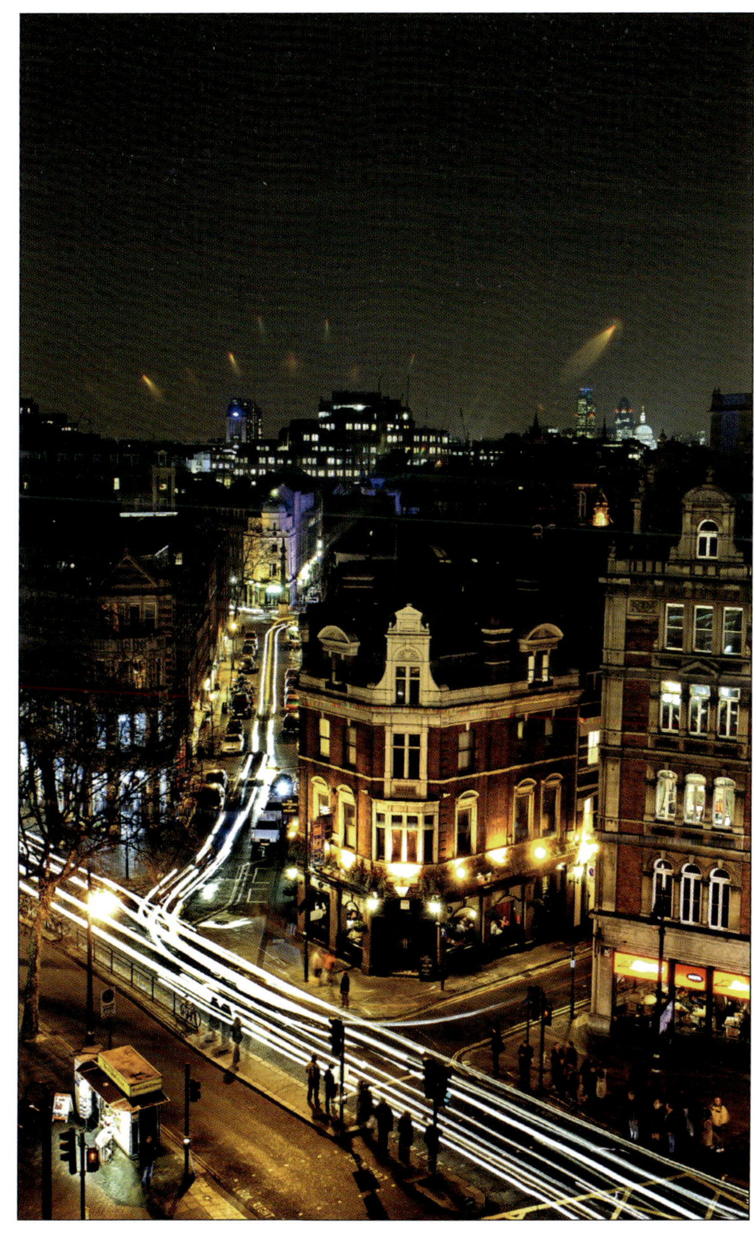

View from Waterloo Bridge at night

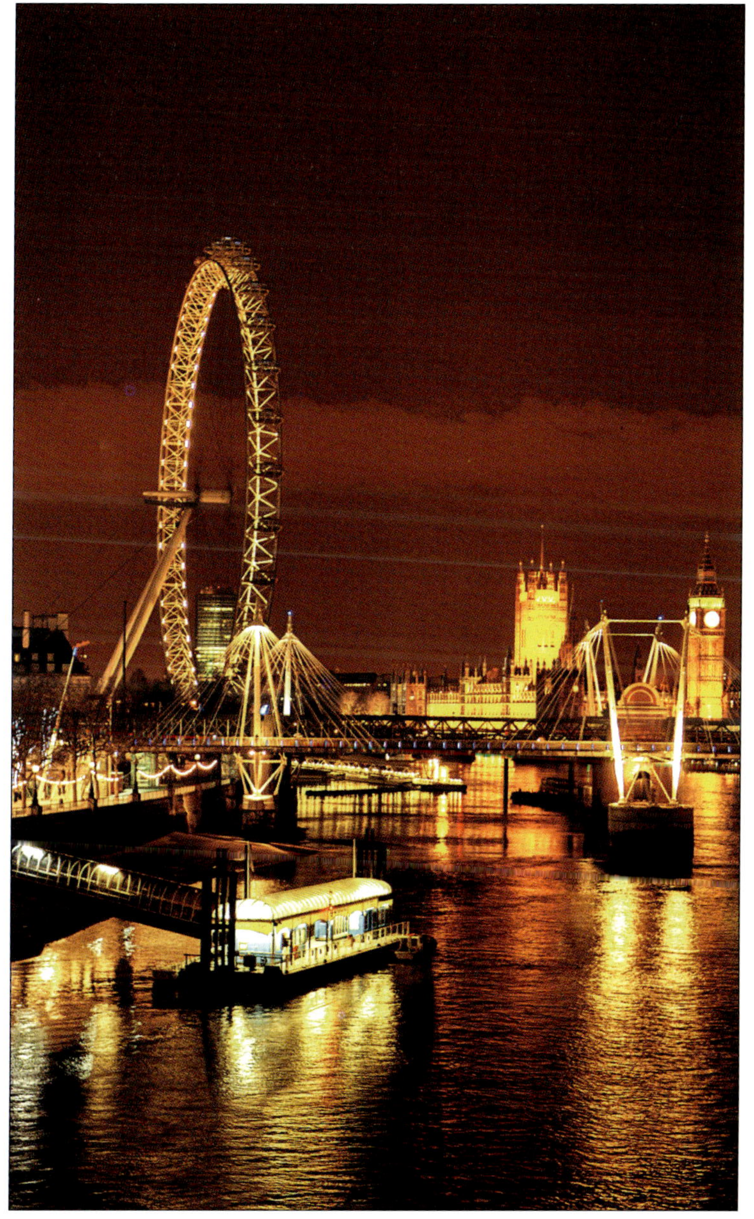

New Concordia Wharf, Southwark

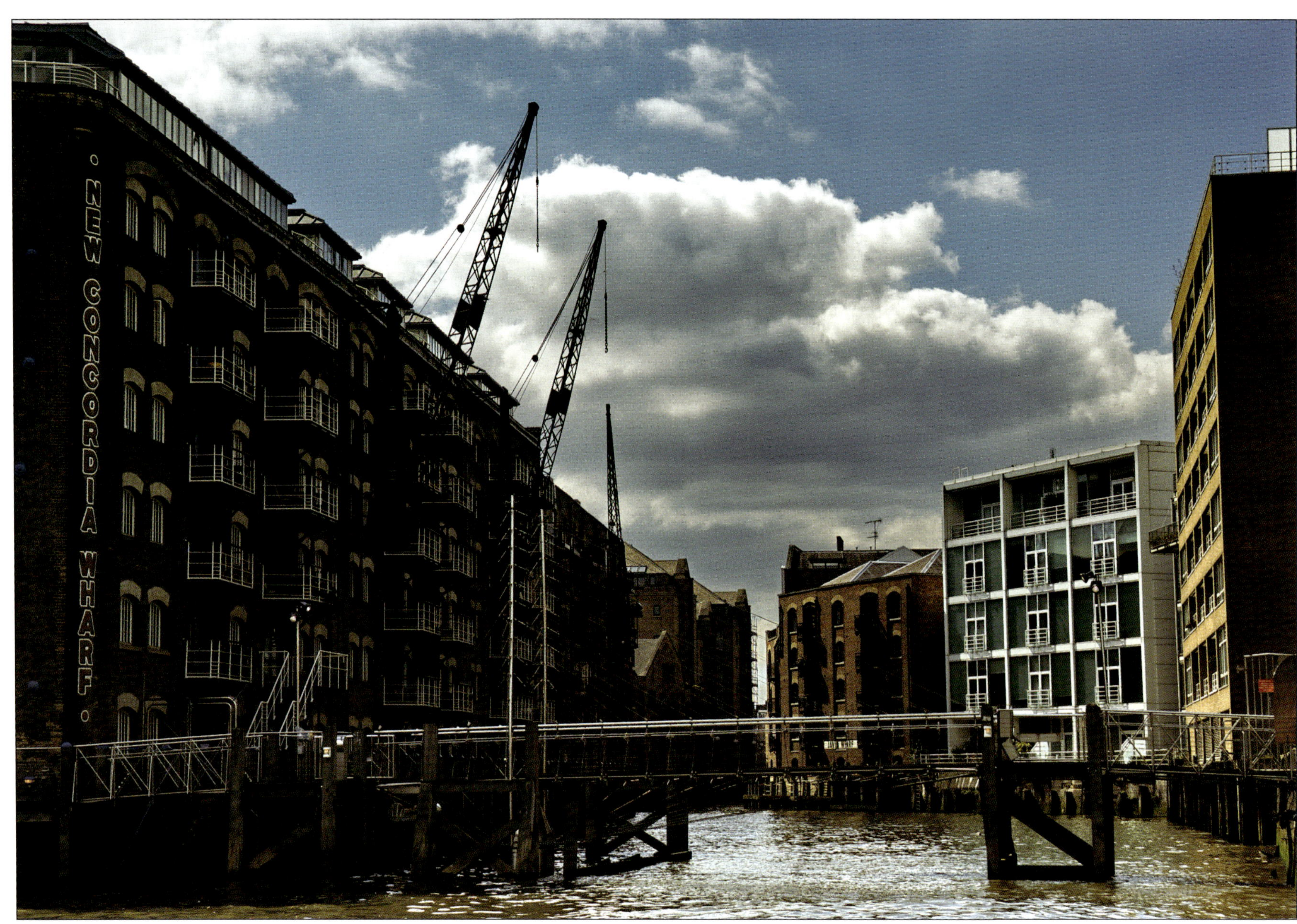

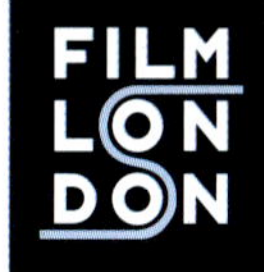
FILM
LONDON

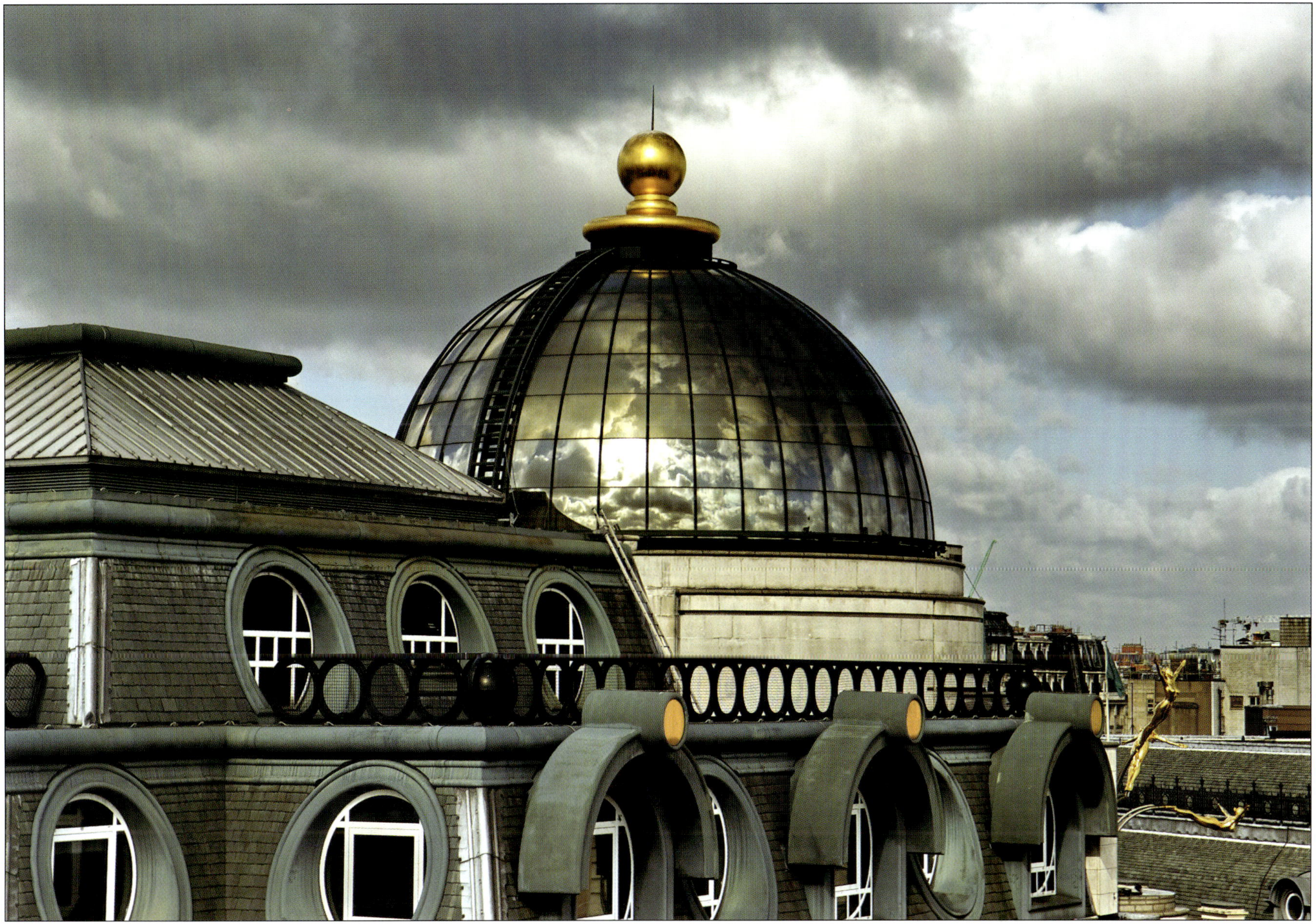

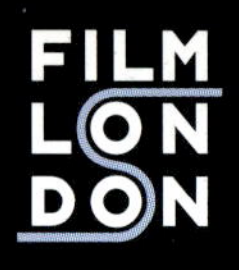

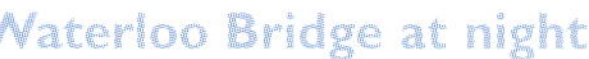

Waterloo Bridge at night

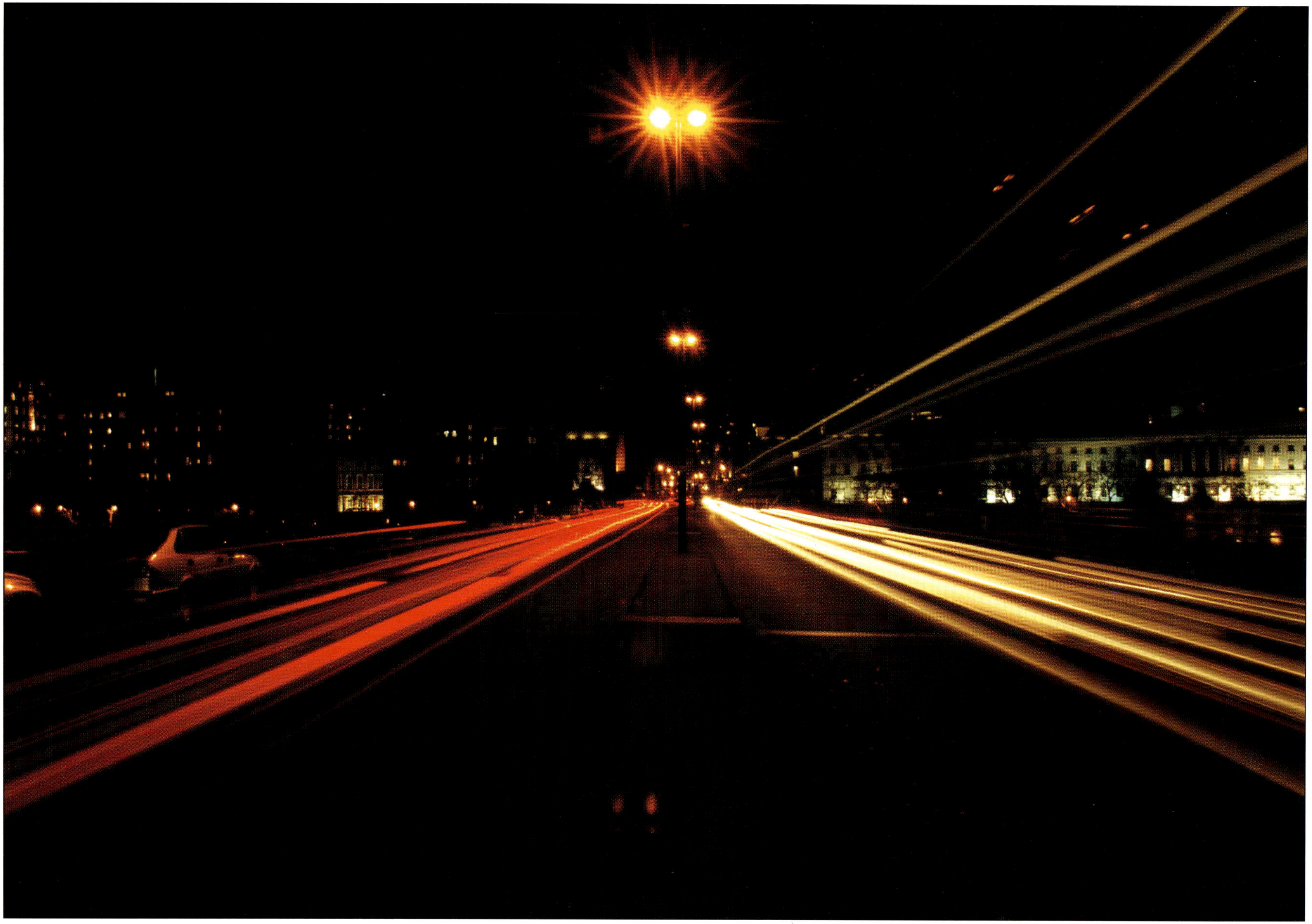

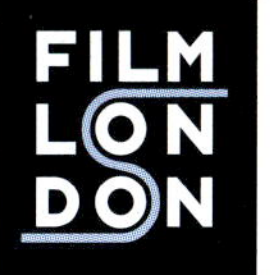

Walker's Court, Soho at dawn

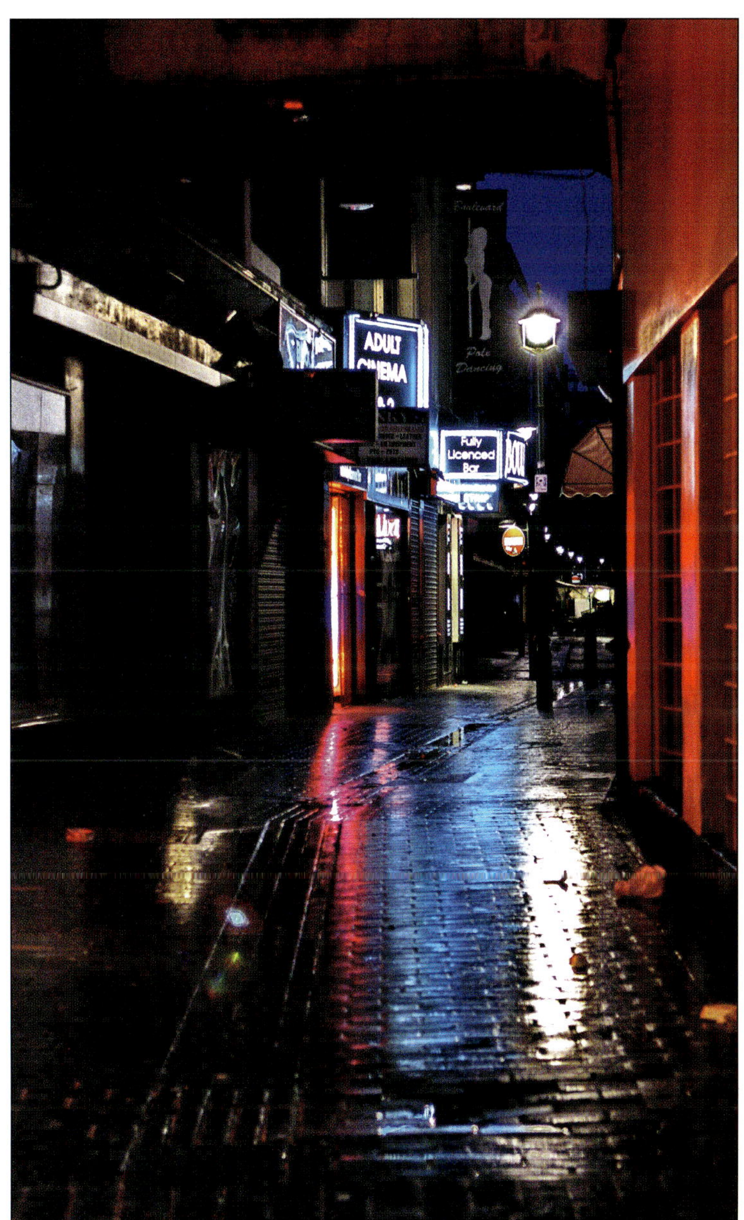

My idea of London was formed by the cinema - the wet streets in *The Blue Lamp*, the red bus in *The Ipcress File*, the frontage of Thomas Crapper & Son in *The Servant*, the Doric medical school in *Doctor in the House*, Harrods Food Hall in *The Pumpkin Eater*, and the bizarre goings-on in an unlikely Notting Hill in *Leo the Last*. You could say, I'm afraid, that the most striking views of London usually came from foreigners - Antonioni for a South London park in *Blow-Up*, Patrice Chéreau for the primary-coloured ugliness of Peckham in *Intimacy*, Roman Polanski for South Kensington in *Repulsion* and Louis Malle for a creamy upper-middle class London in *Damage*. A new generation needs to find London for itself, and how better than through the indelible medium of film?

David Hare

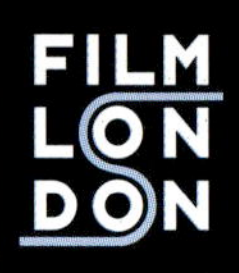

Bow Street at dawn

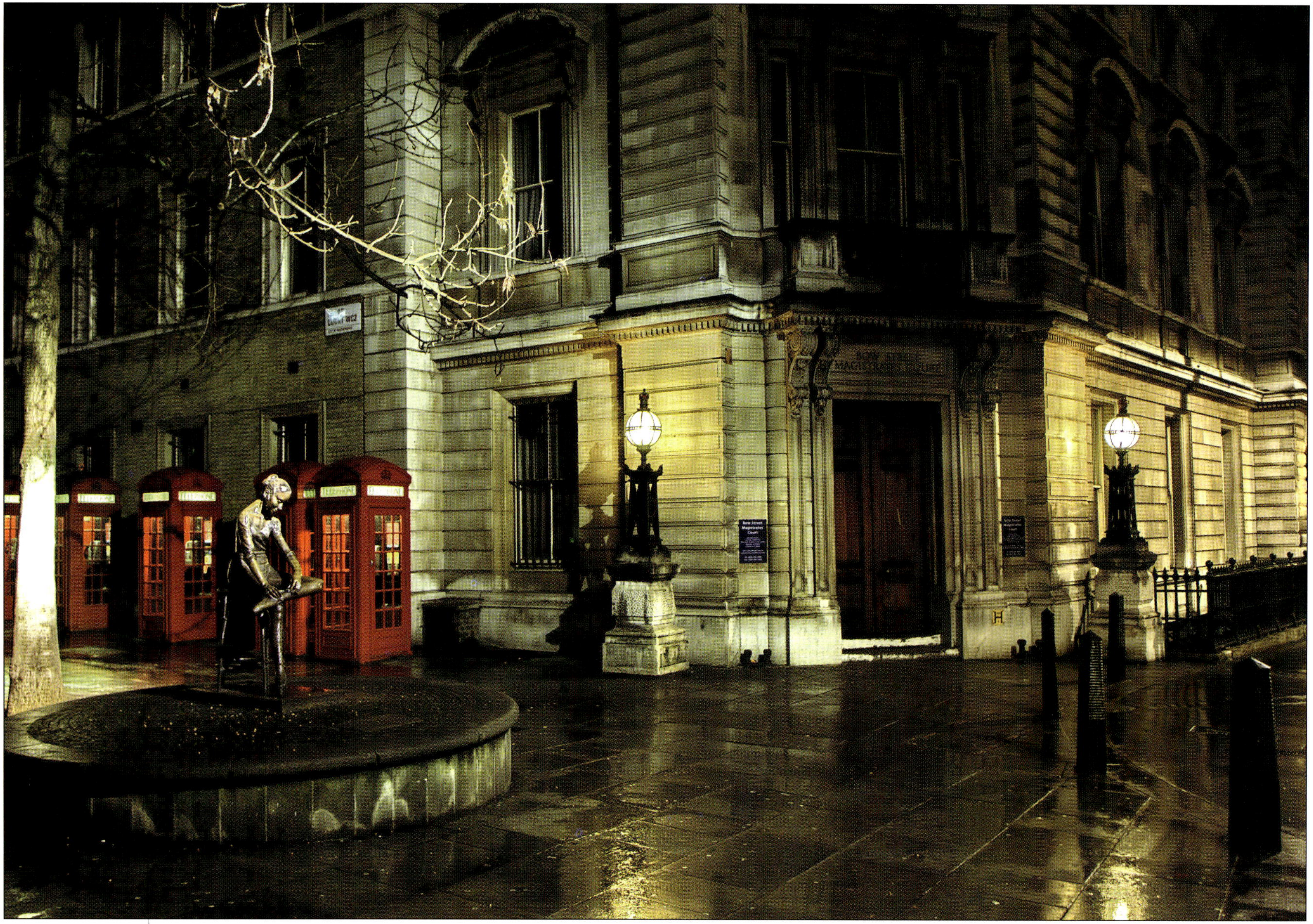

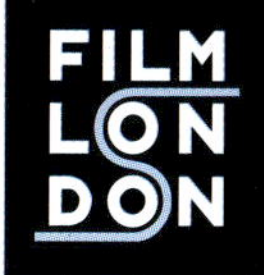
FILM
LON
DON

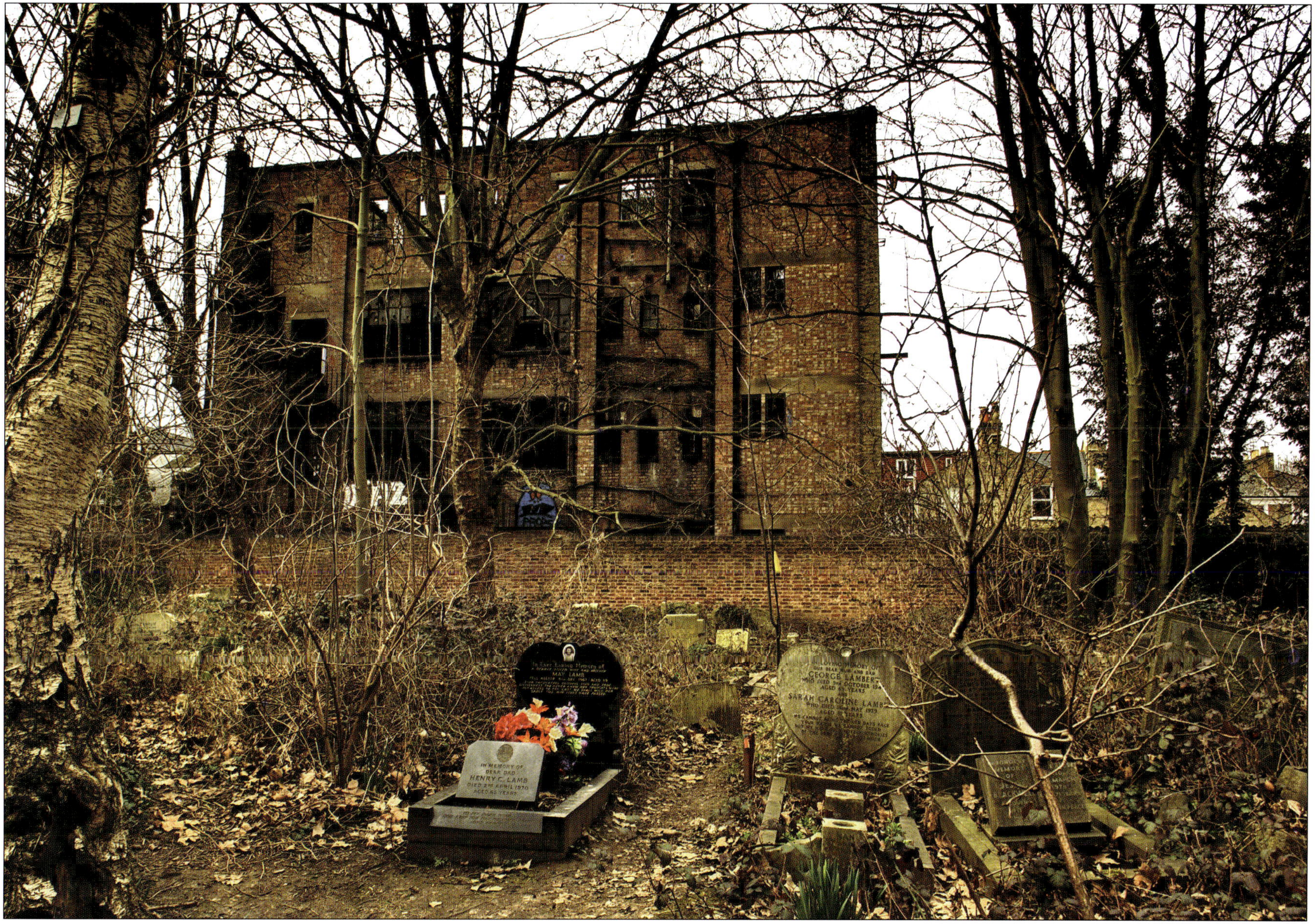

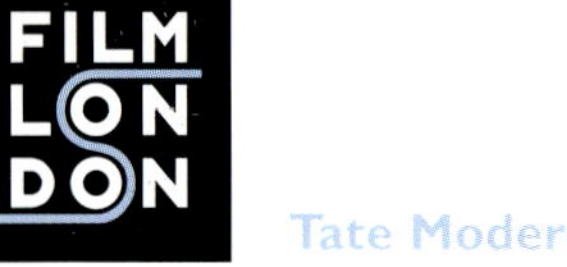

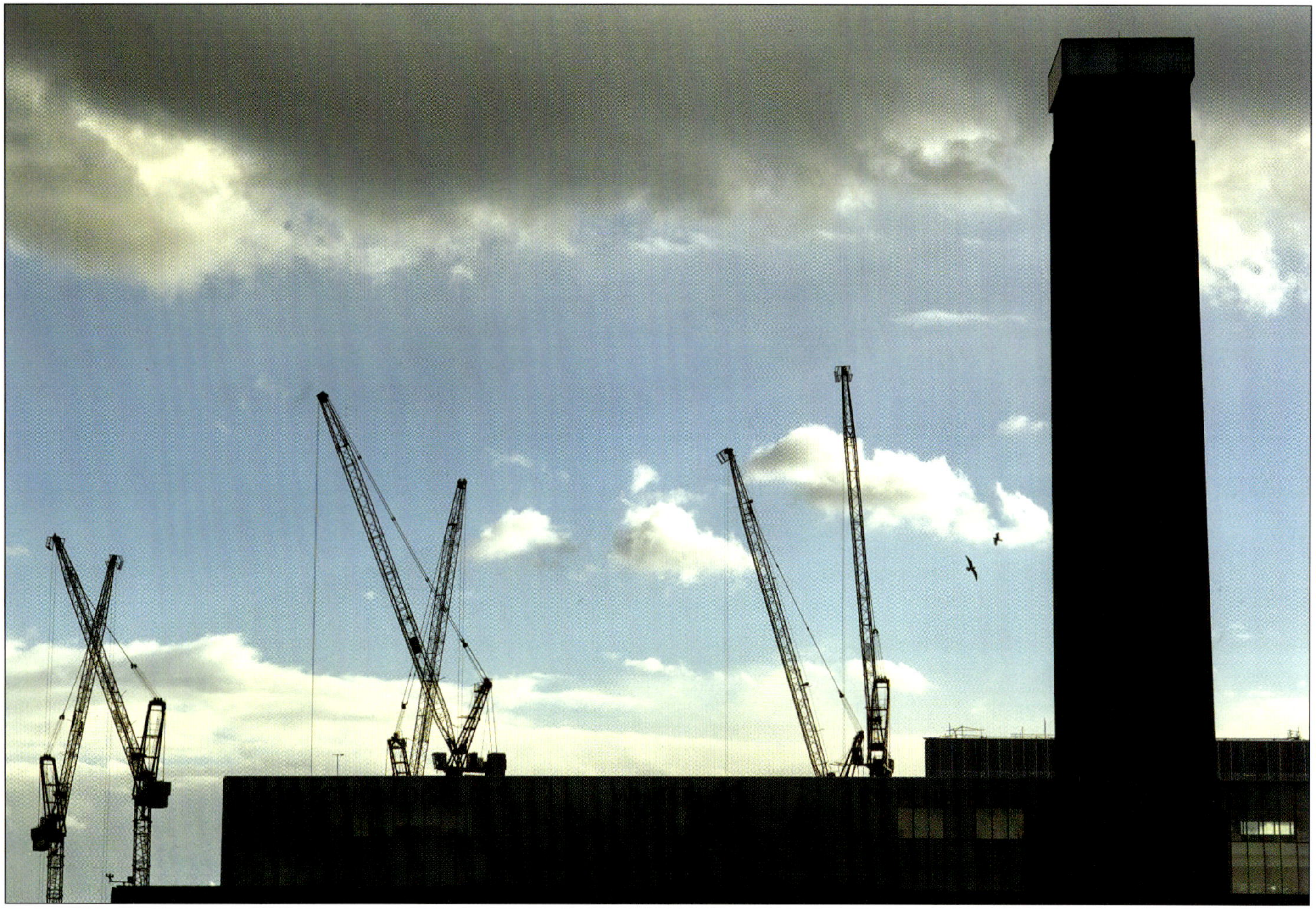

Shooting in London is a pleasure. The crews are wonderful. The city is film-friendly and cooperative. And, for someone like myself, the weather is ideal.

Woody Allen

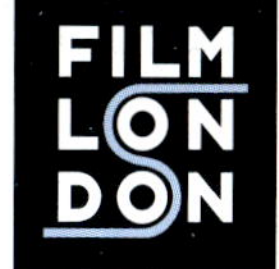

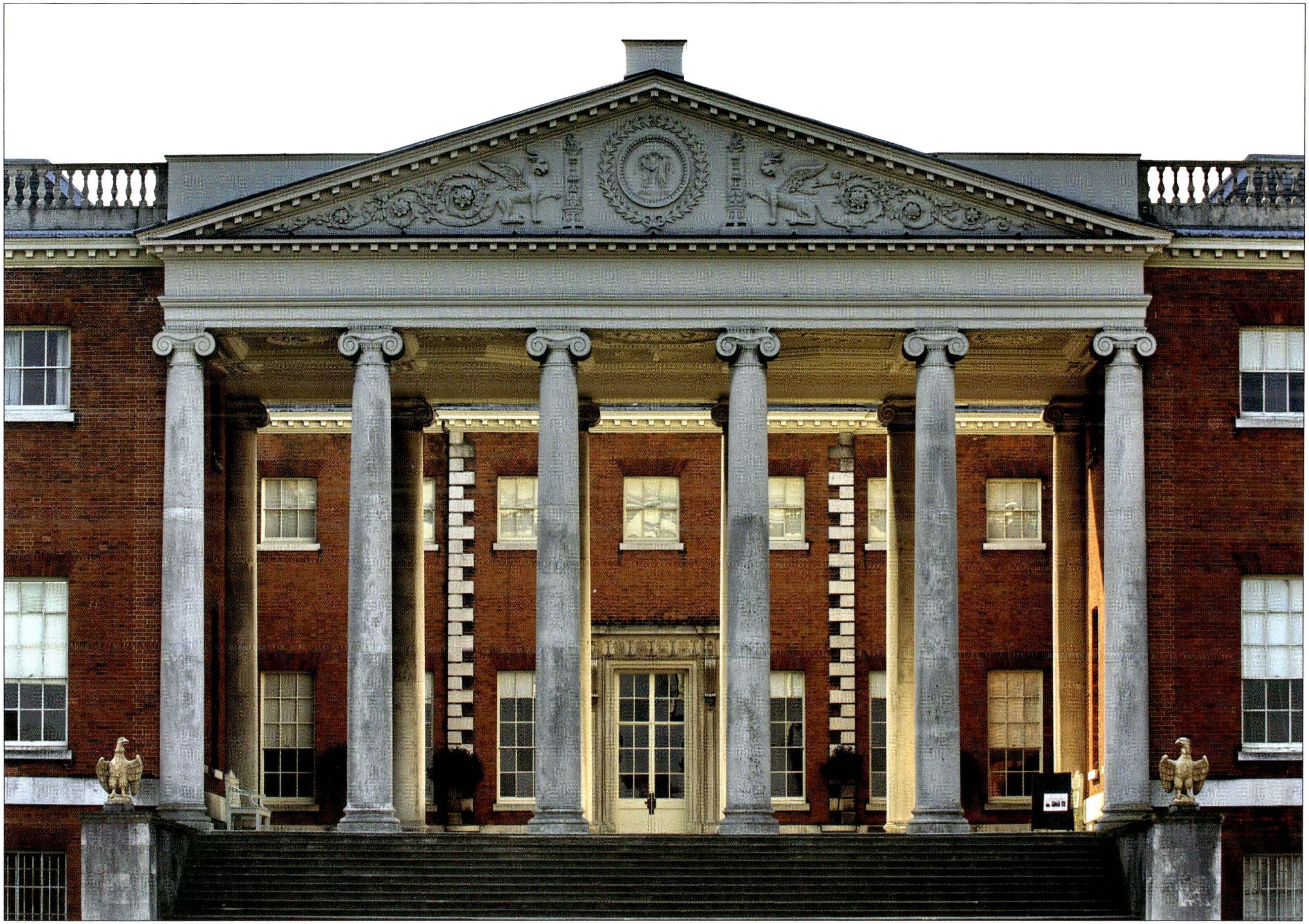

Osterley Park, Hounslow

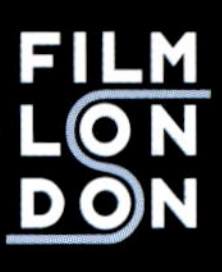
FILM
LON
DON

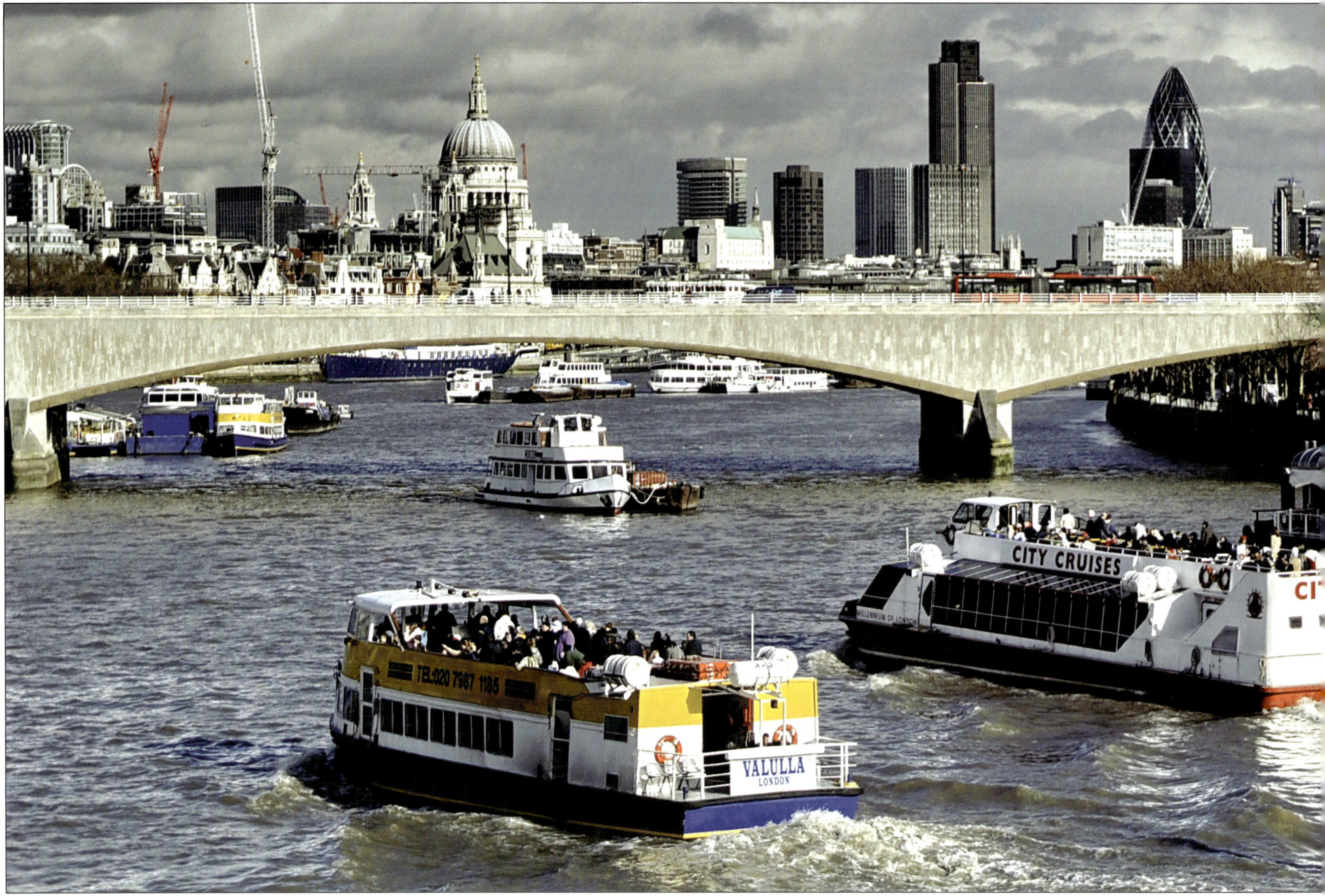

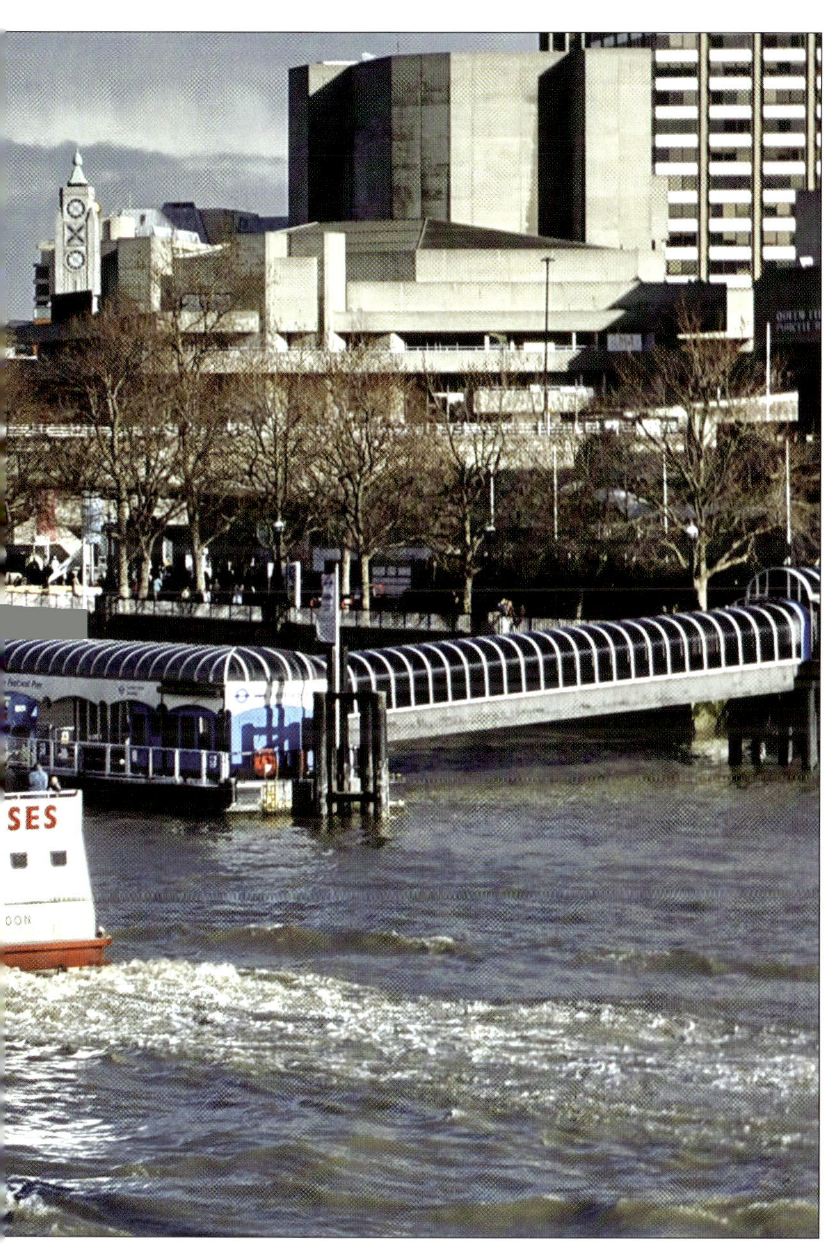

The last line of my film *Alfie* 'What's it all about?' was said on Waterloo Bridge, which was a great location for the end of the film with incredible views up and down the river which, by the way, have changed almost beyond recognition in the 40 years since we made the film. For me, however, Waterloo Bridge was not only a wonderful location, it had at that time for at least 25 years been an integral part of my life. As a young man I lived at the Elephant and Castle and Waterloo Bridge was the gateway to the glamour and bright lights of the West End. I have walked over that bridge a thousand times, always with great pleasure. It was like a frontier crossing from where I came from to where I wanted to go. The last shot was in the middle of the bridge and instead of walking back to the Elephant and Castle, I got into a chauffeur-driven car to my home in the West End. I love this bridge and I never cross it without mixed emotions.

Sir Michael Caine CBE

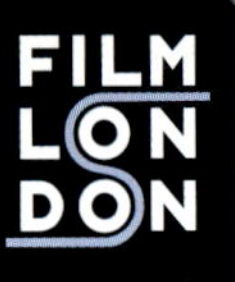

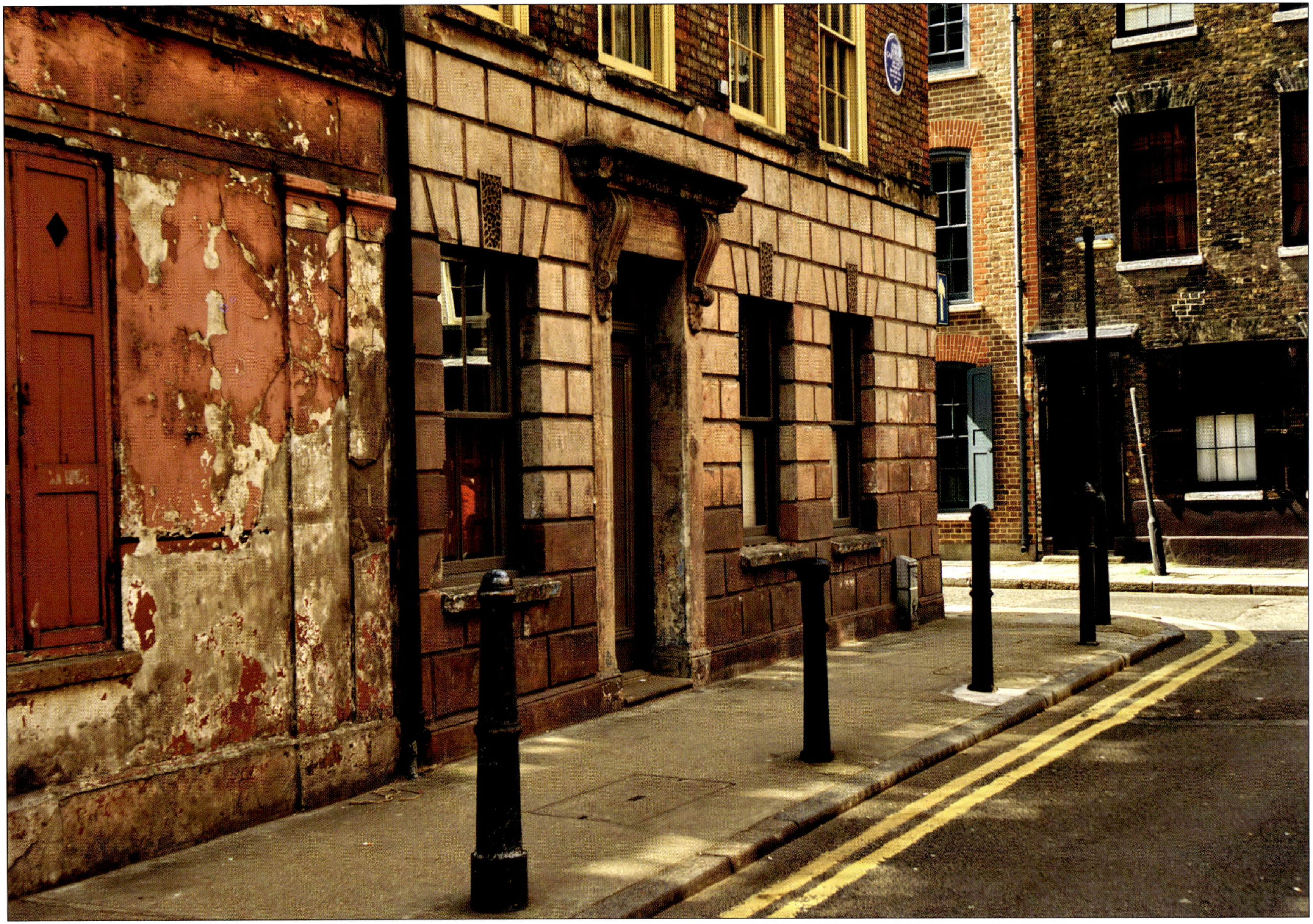

Princelet Street, Tower Hamlets

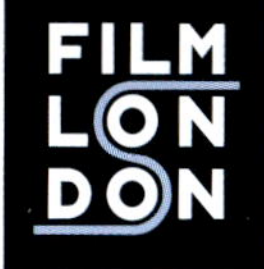

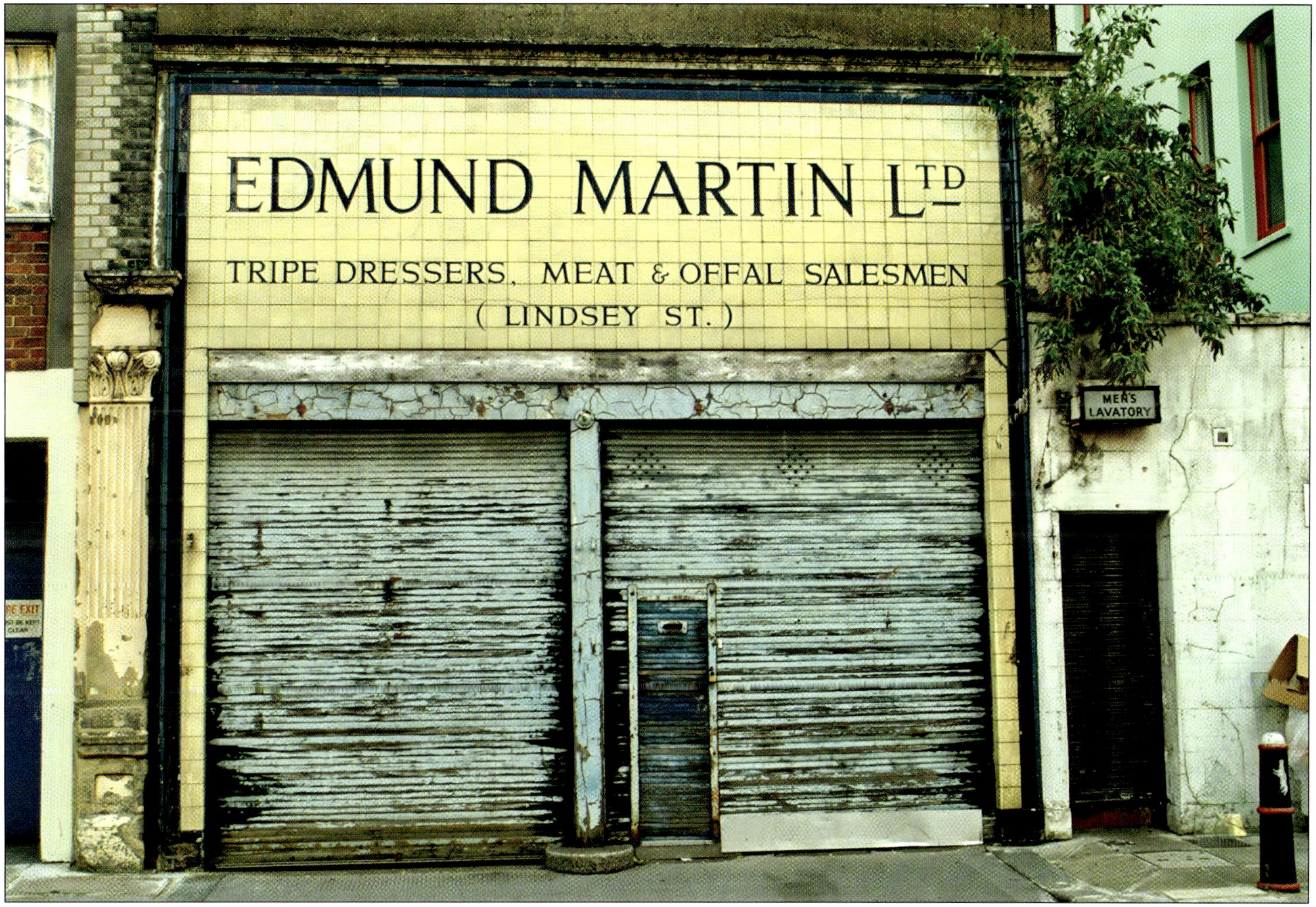

I was immediately taken by the romance of Ealing Studios, its history, its intimacy - the sense of a Hollywood studio in miniature, and I still feel that every day I am there. It has produced some of the best loved British classics and London set movies of all time, *The Man in the White Suit, Passport to Pimlico, The Ladykillers, The Lavender Hill Mob.* Witty, eccentric, funny, sad. Testimonies to a unique British glamour and a unique British spirit.

Barnaby Thompson

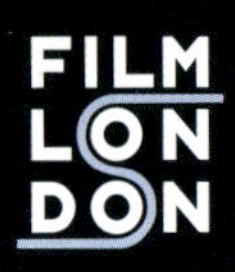
FILM
LON
DON

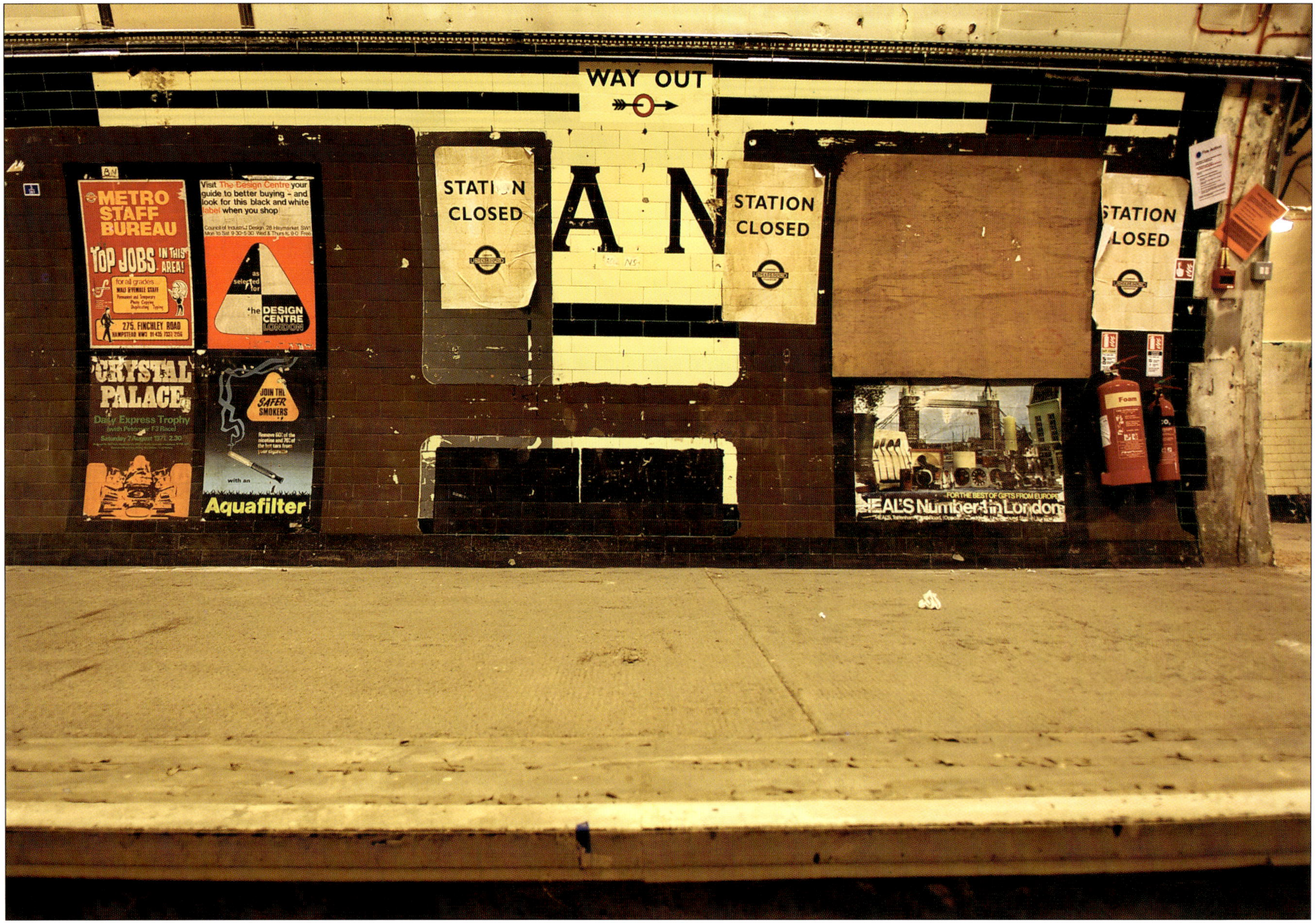

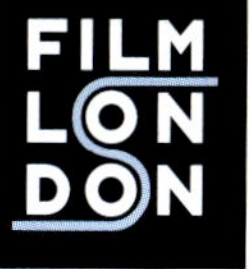

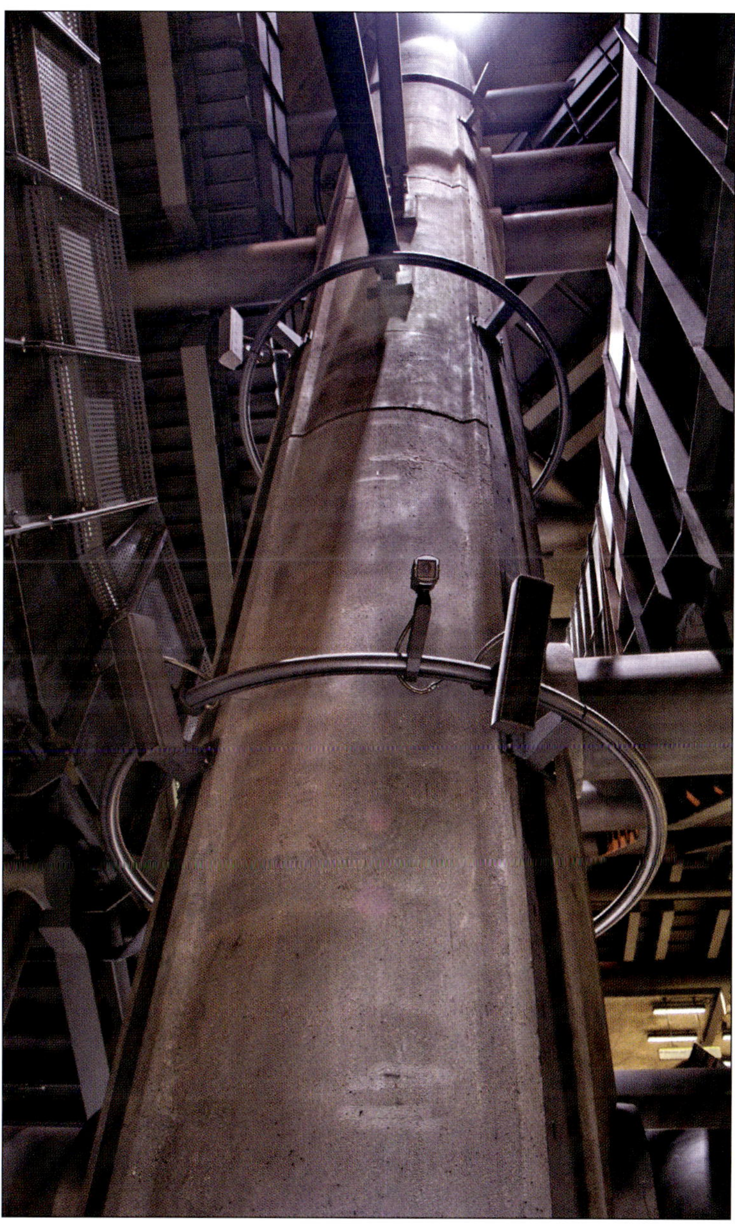

People are always fascinated by what lies beneath, particularly in London. We don't really know what's below us. There's so much history beneath our feet. The great thing about the tube as a location is that you're completely isolated from the outside world. It's like *The Poseidon Adventure* or *Alien*. You might as well be in outer space or at the bottom of the sea.

Christopher Smith

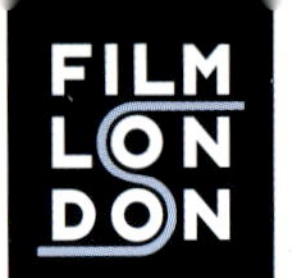
FILM
LONDON

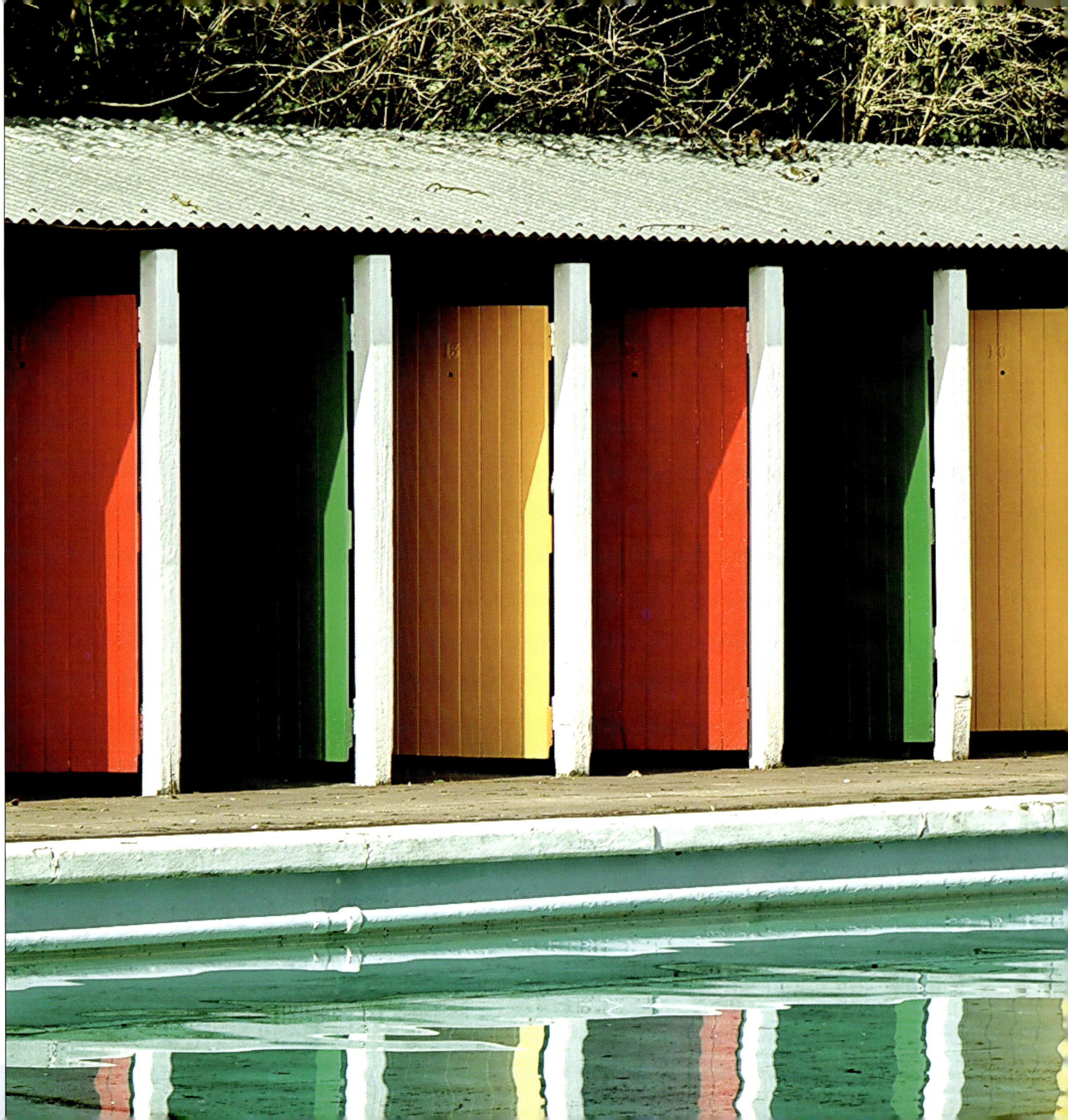

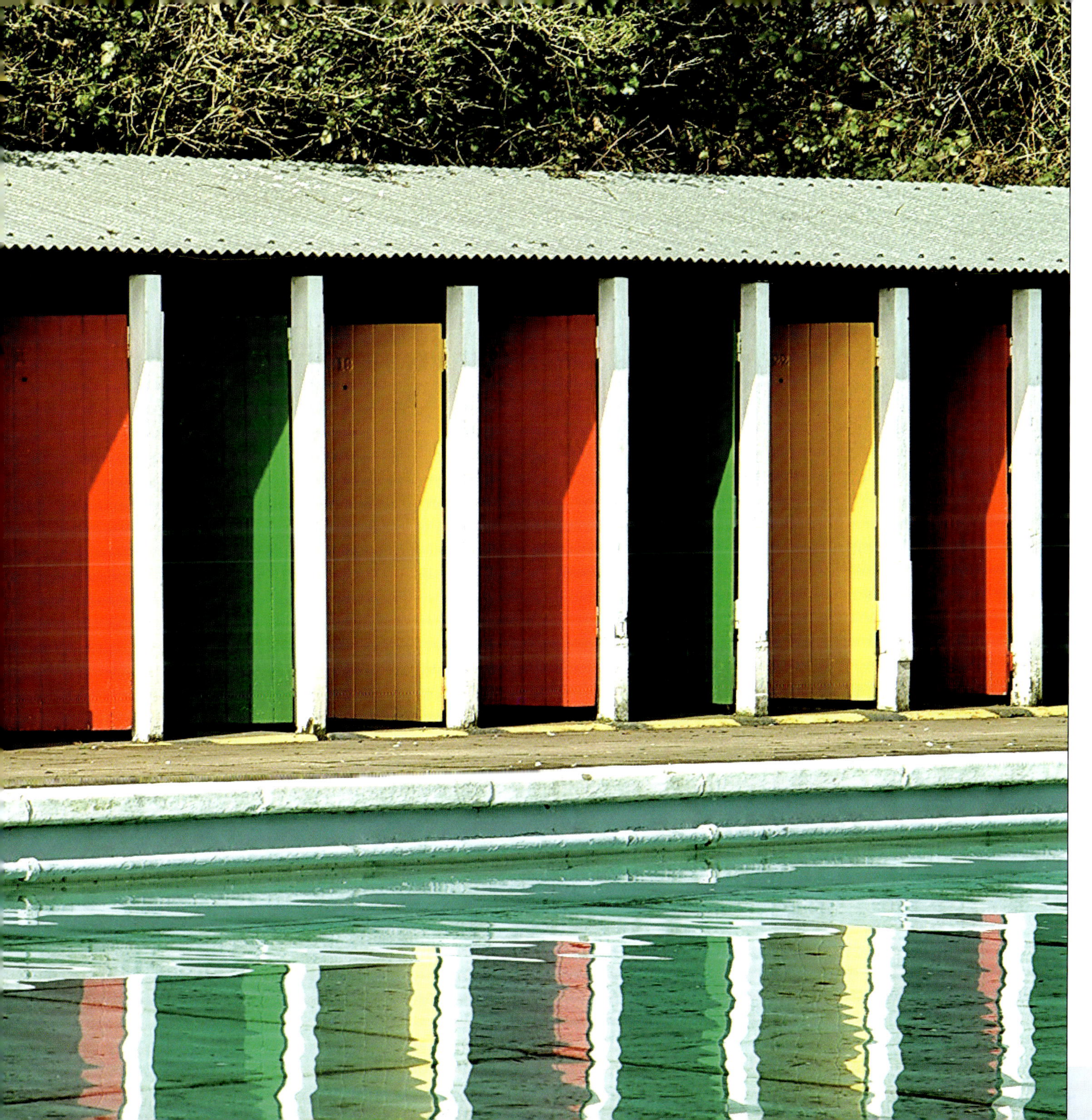

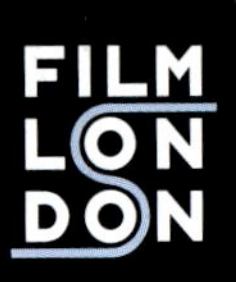

The Thames at low tide, Wapping

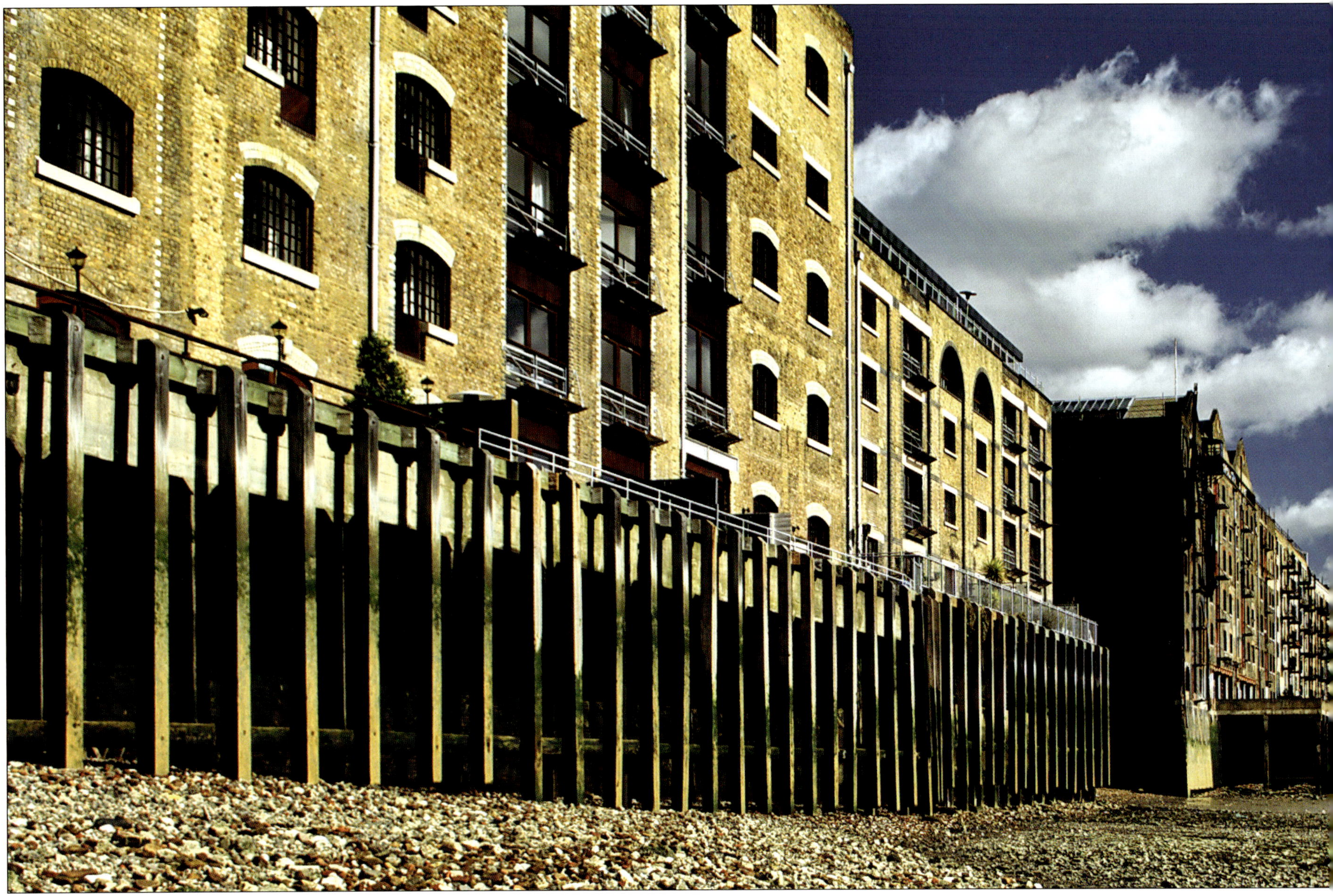

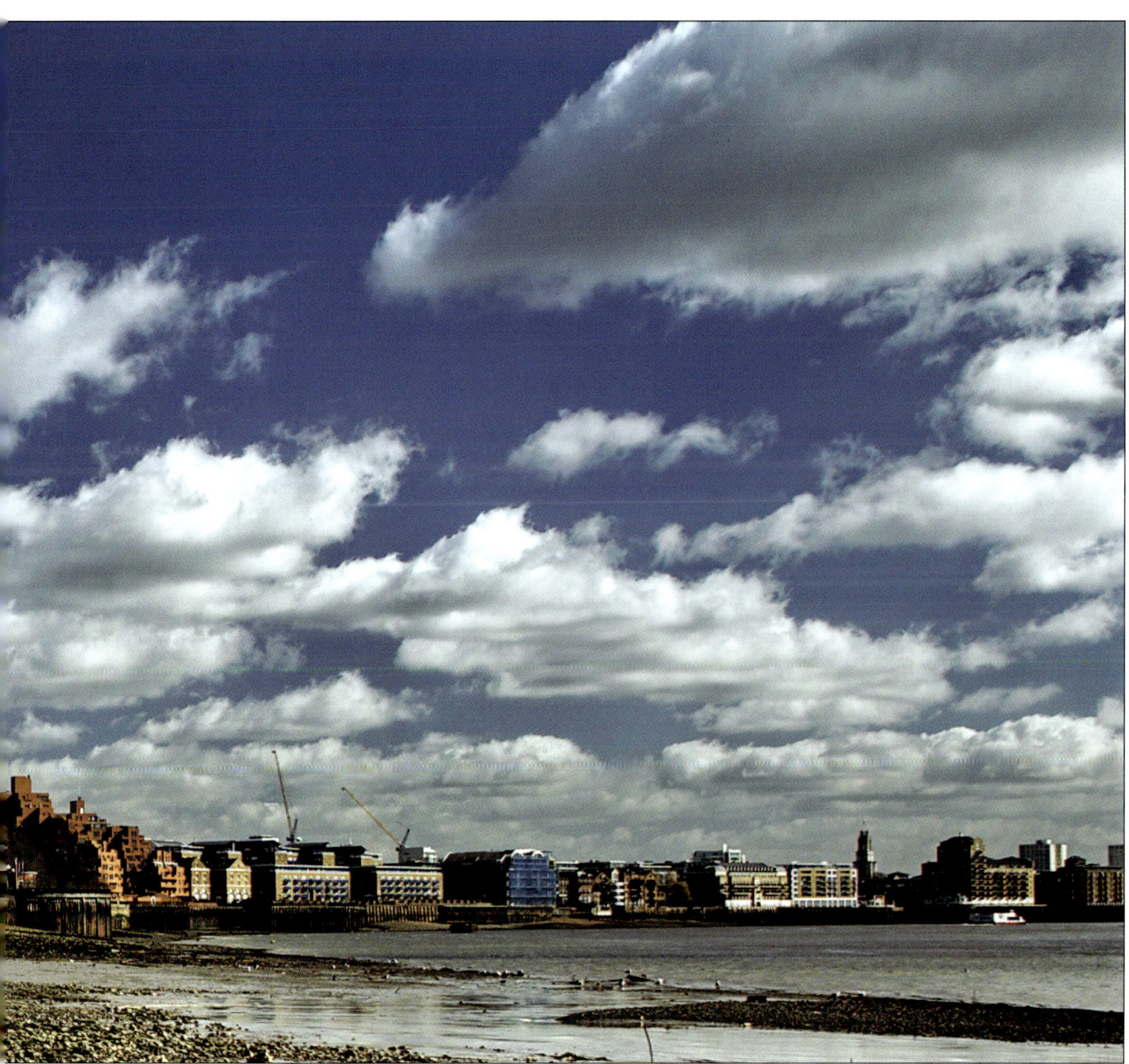

London will always offer unexpected solutions. *Shakespeare in Love* locations were tough - the Globe was out - unaffordable, and anyway not 'the Rose', and Elizabethan London has all but disappeared. What was definitely there, unchanged, was the river - though the embankments of course had, and everyone thought we should do those scenes on a tank at Shepperton. I thought the scale would be hopelessly restricted, and CGI was then relatively new and far too expensive. Hammersmith Bridge was closed at the time, and west Londoners had to drive over Chiswick Bridge and through Mortlake to go south. I kept seeing this stretch of river that I thought must be able to stand for the Elizabethan Thames. So we built a set under Barnes Bridge, which became London Bridge, and Twickenham became Wapping. With some judicious editing, we had the Thames on our backlot. So much is possible in London if you look.

John Madden

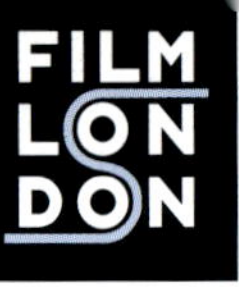

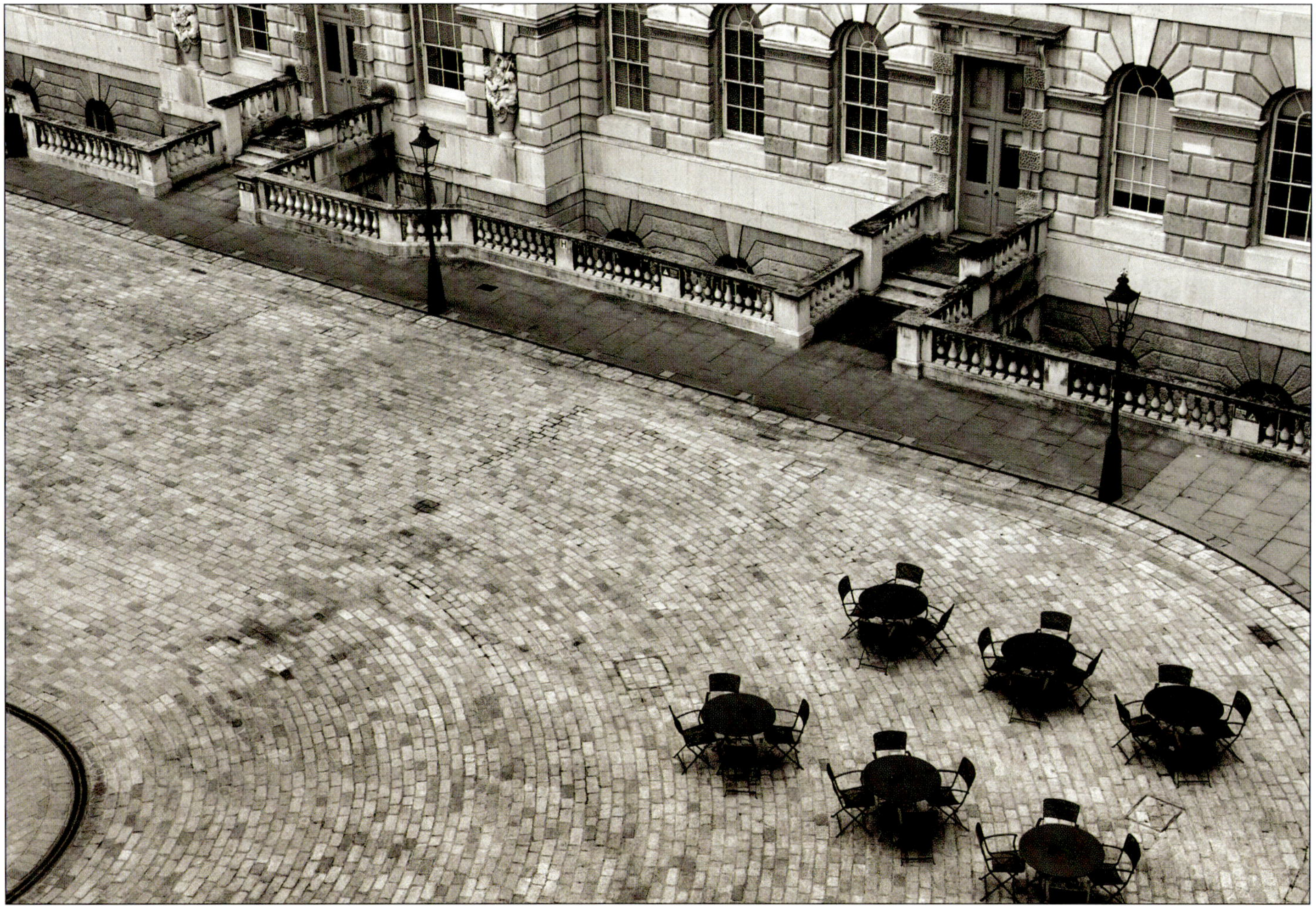

Courtyard and East Façade at Somerset House

London is the greatest city for human stories in the world. It seethes with narrative and mystery with comedy, tragedy, despair and an ecstasy not always produced by chemical means... I feel as though you could pick up any thread and it would lead you through the labyrinth to the heart of life.

Emma Thompson

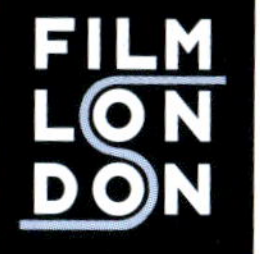

View from the roof of the Palace Theatre

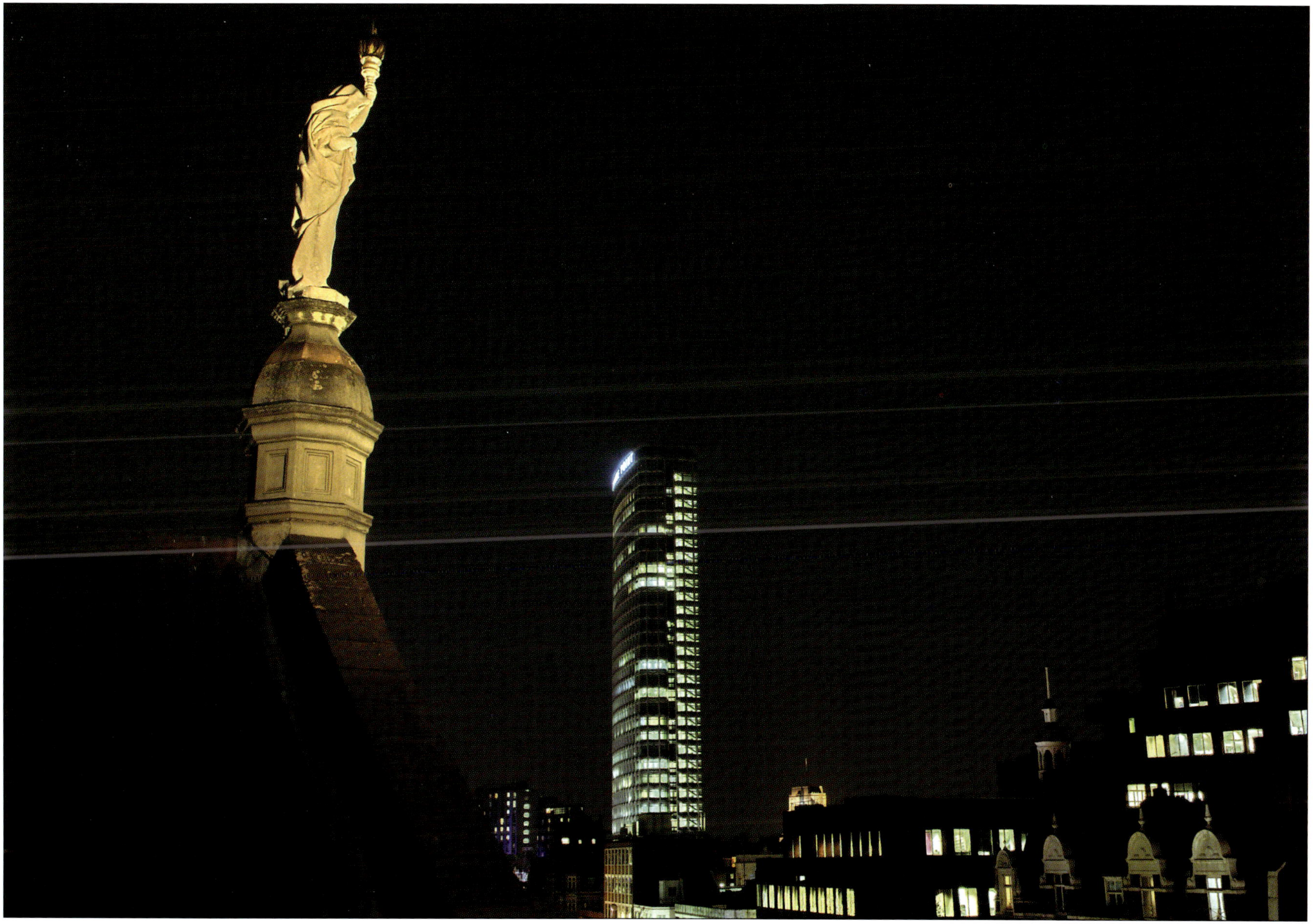

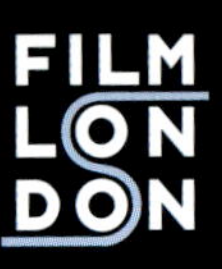

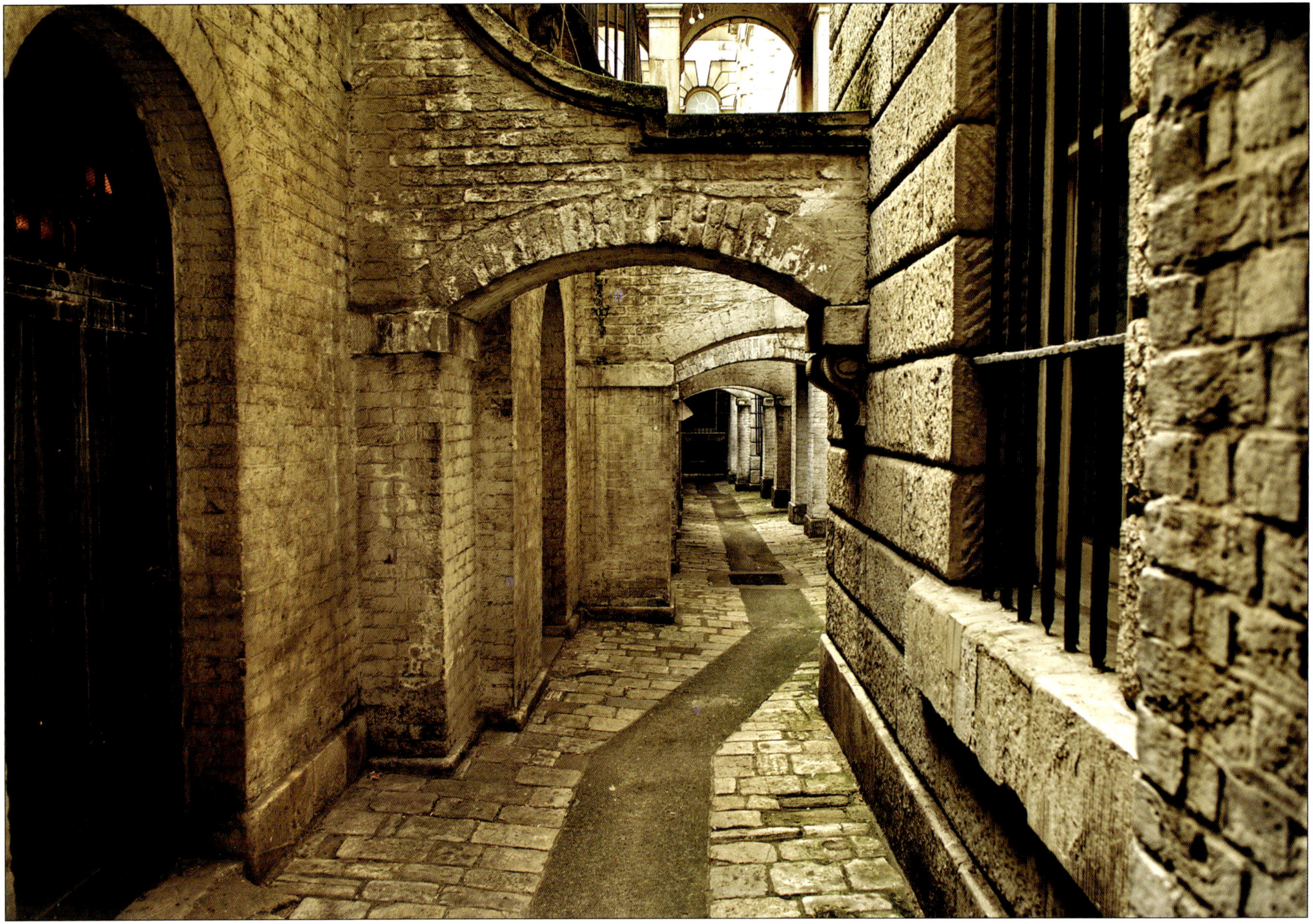

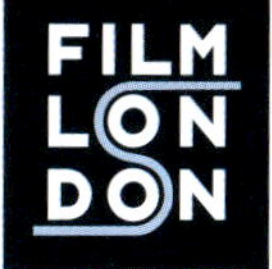

It's interesting to note that so many films that are now memorable explore the dark bitter heart of our town - *Naked*, *Peeping Tom*, *Frenzy*, *Love is The Devil*, *10 Rillington Place*, *Out of Control* and *Bullet Boy* amongst others all portray a London of carnal and bestial qualities, even the comedic *Withnail & I* and the original *Alfie* conceal an ice-cold sucker punch. Whatever the reason, from Hitchcock to Maybury we have shown a determined spirit to open up the darkness and real London lovers like Stephen Frears with movies like *Prick Up Your Ears*, *Dirty Pretty Things* and *My Beautiful Laundrette* have revelled in its noirish landscape and its wealth of chilling yarns.

Stephen Woolley

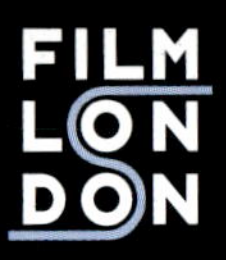
FILM
LON
DON

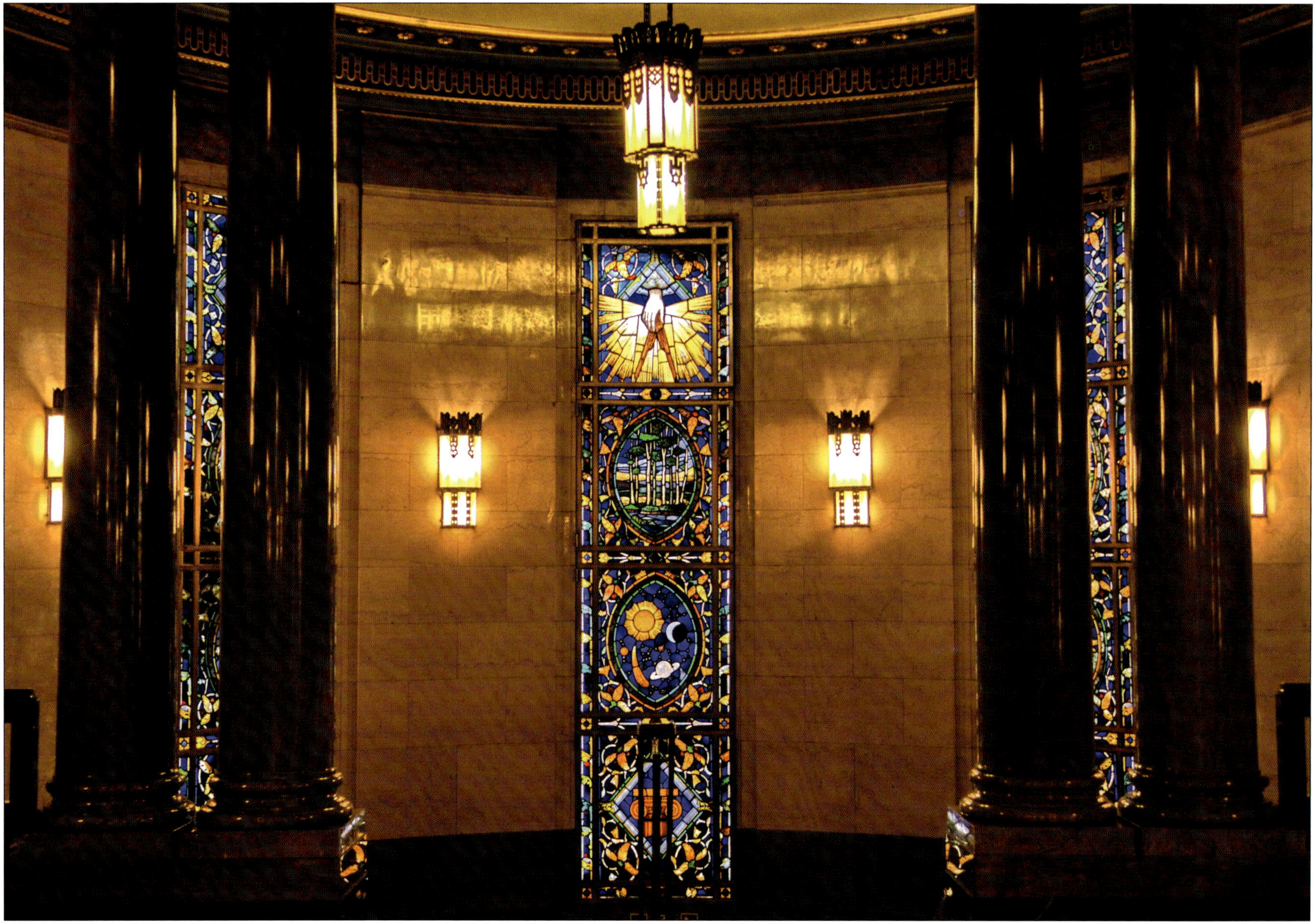

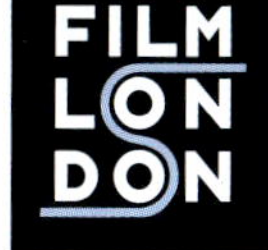

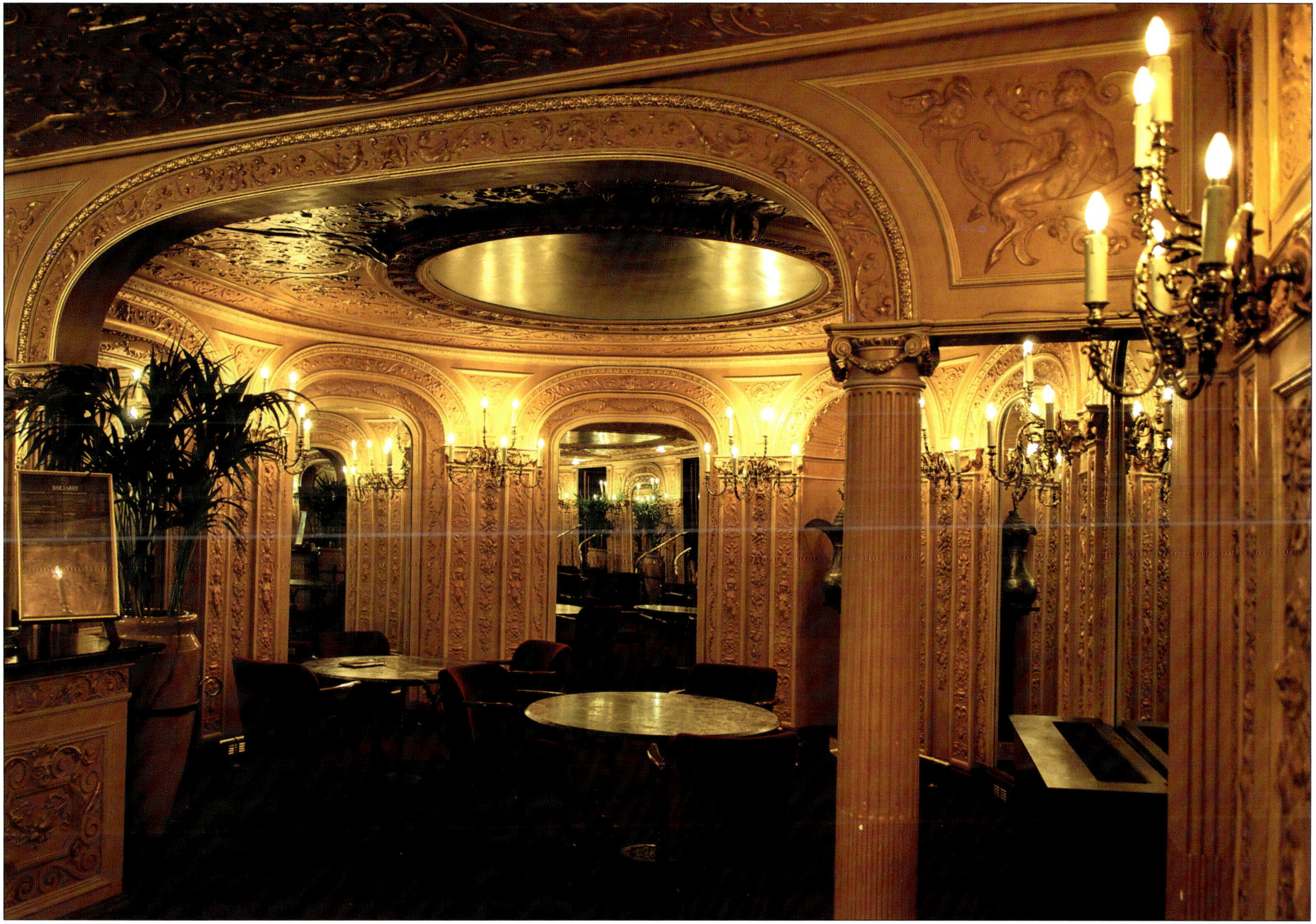

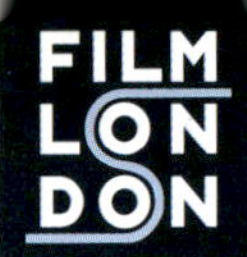

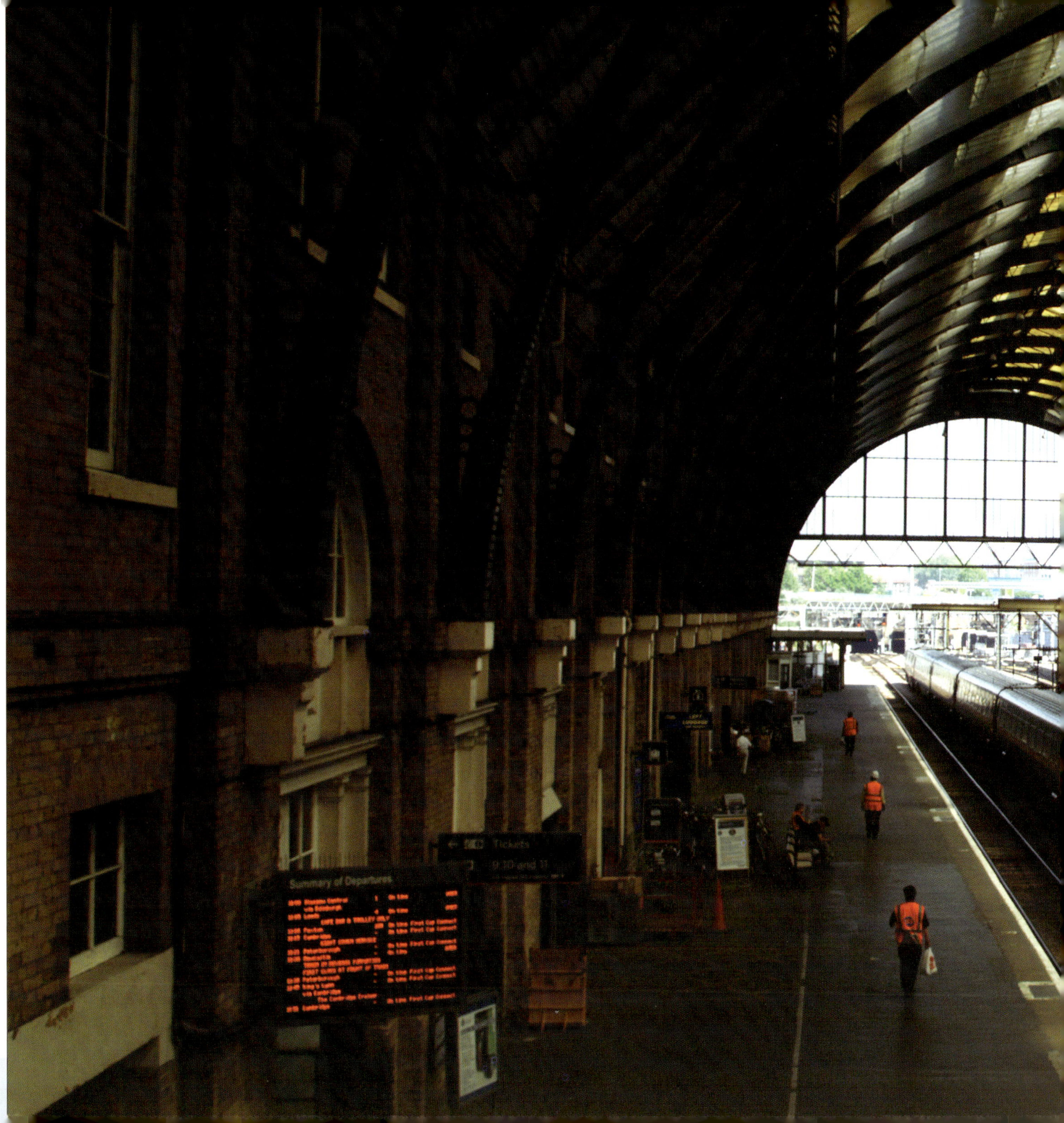

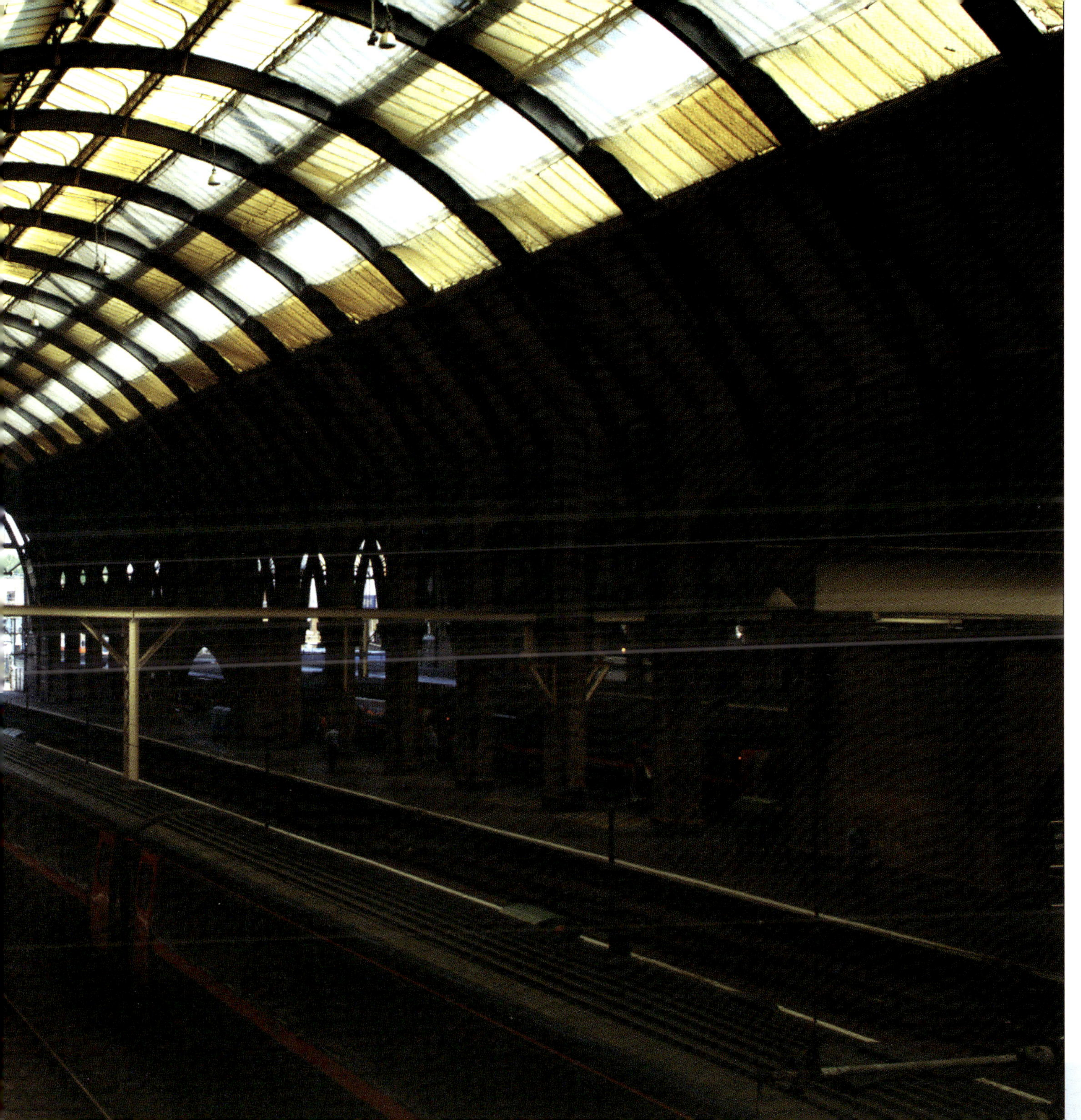

For me... King's Cross Station is a very, very romantic place, probably the most romantic station, purely because my parents met here. So, that's always been part of my childhood folklore. My dad had just joined the navy, my mum had just joined the Wrens, they were both travelling up to Arbroath in Scotland from London and they met on the train pulling out of King's Cross. So, I wanted Harry to go to Hogwarts by train – I just love trains, I'm a bit nerdy like that. And obviously, therefore, it had to be from King's Cross.

JK Rowling

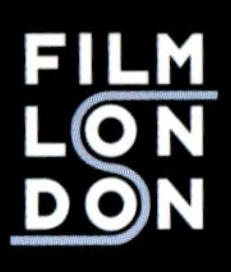
FILM
LON
DON

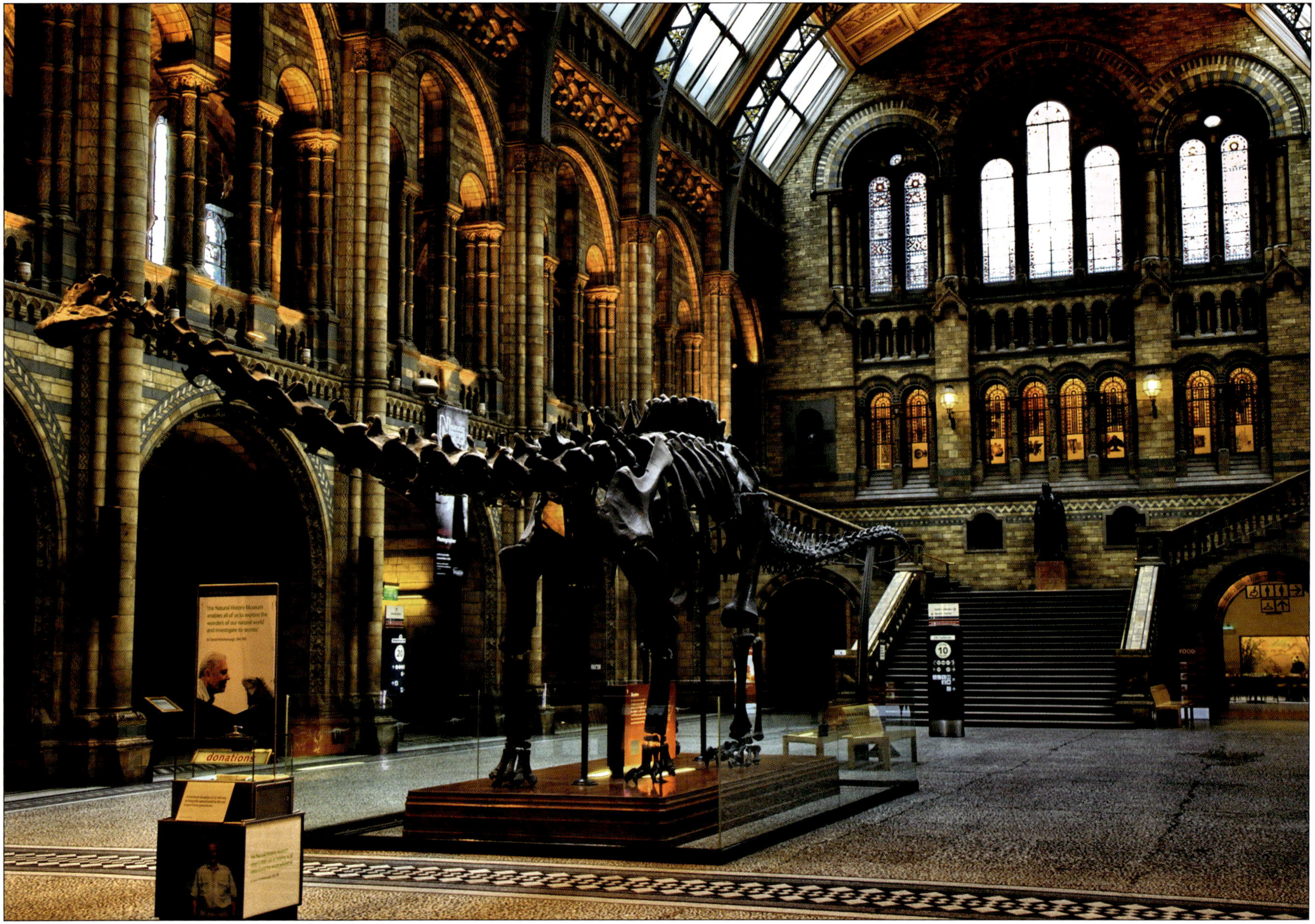

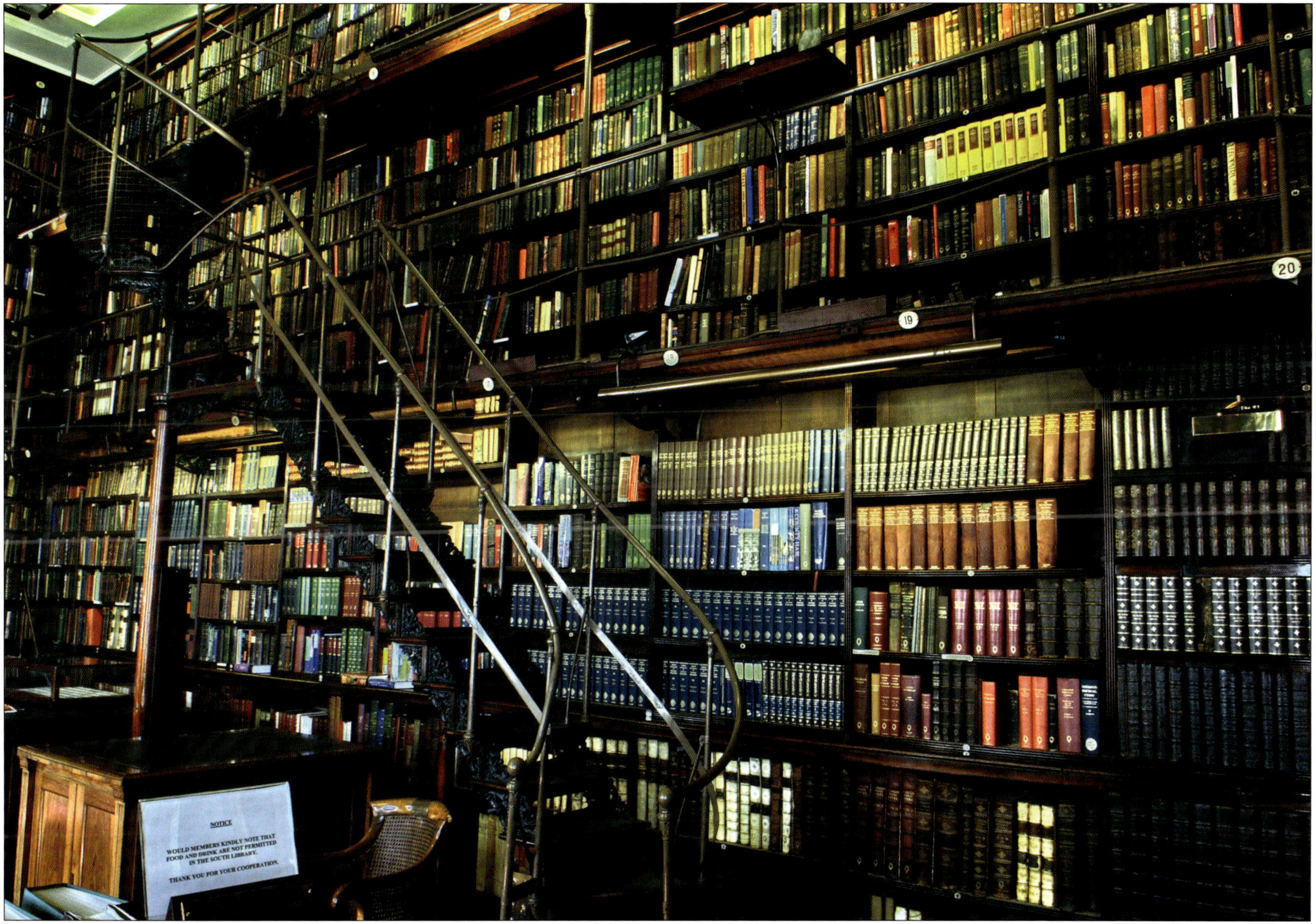
NOTICE
WOULD MEMBERS KINDLY NOTE THAT FOOD AND DRINK ARE NOT PERMITTED IN THE SOUTH LIBRARY.
THANK YOU FOR YOUR COOPERATION.
20
19

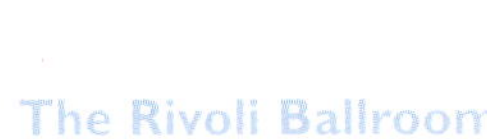

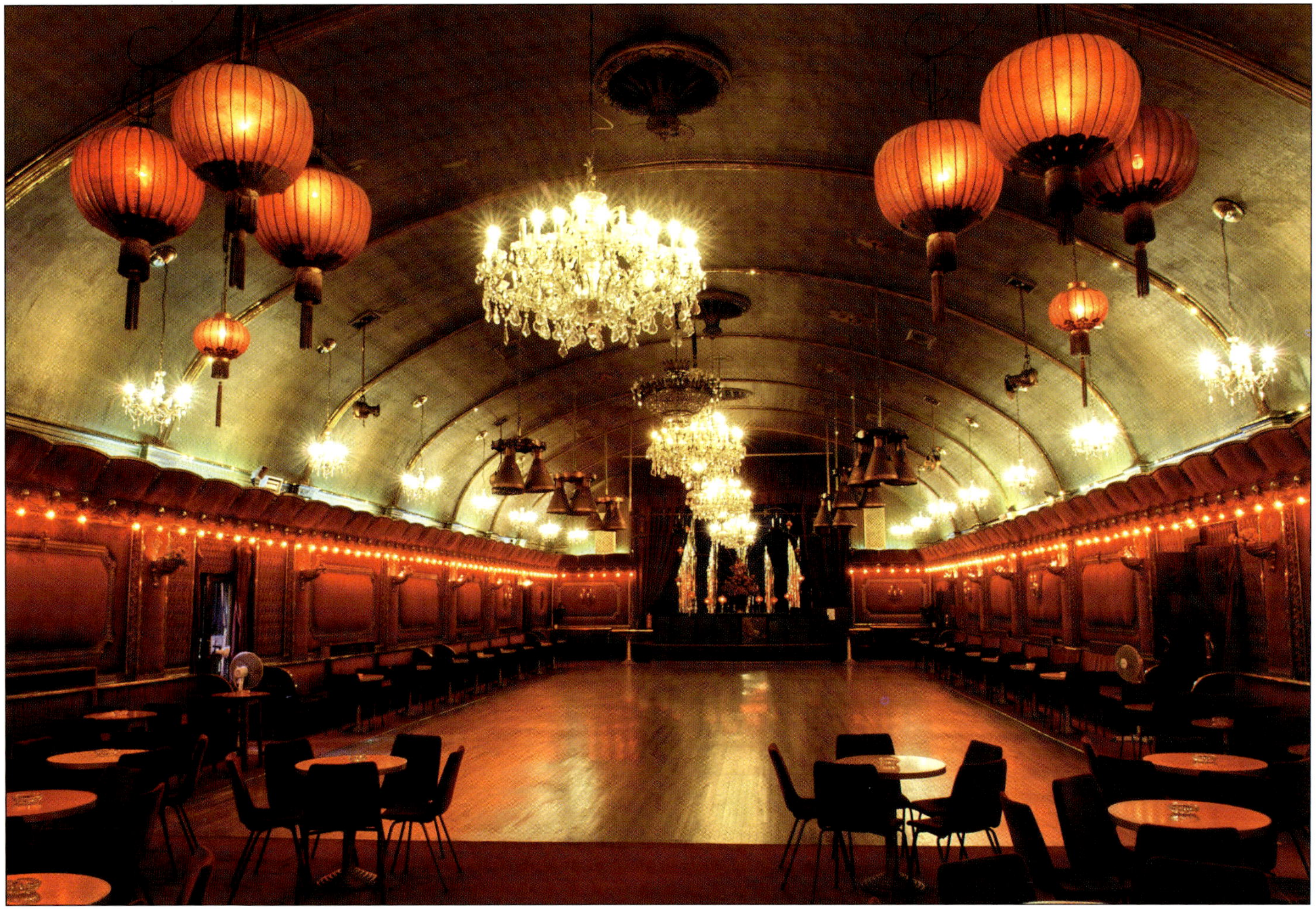

London becomes a universal world, in which you can tell any kind of story.

Mike Leigh

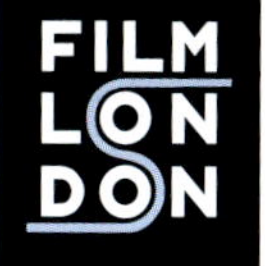

Covent Garden at dawn

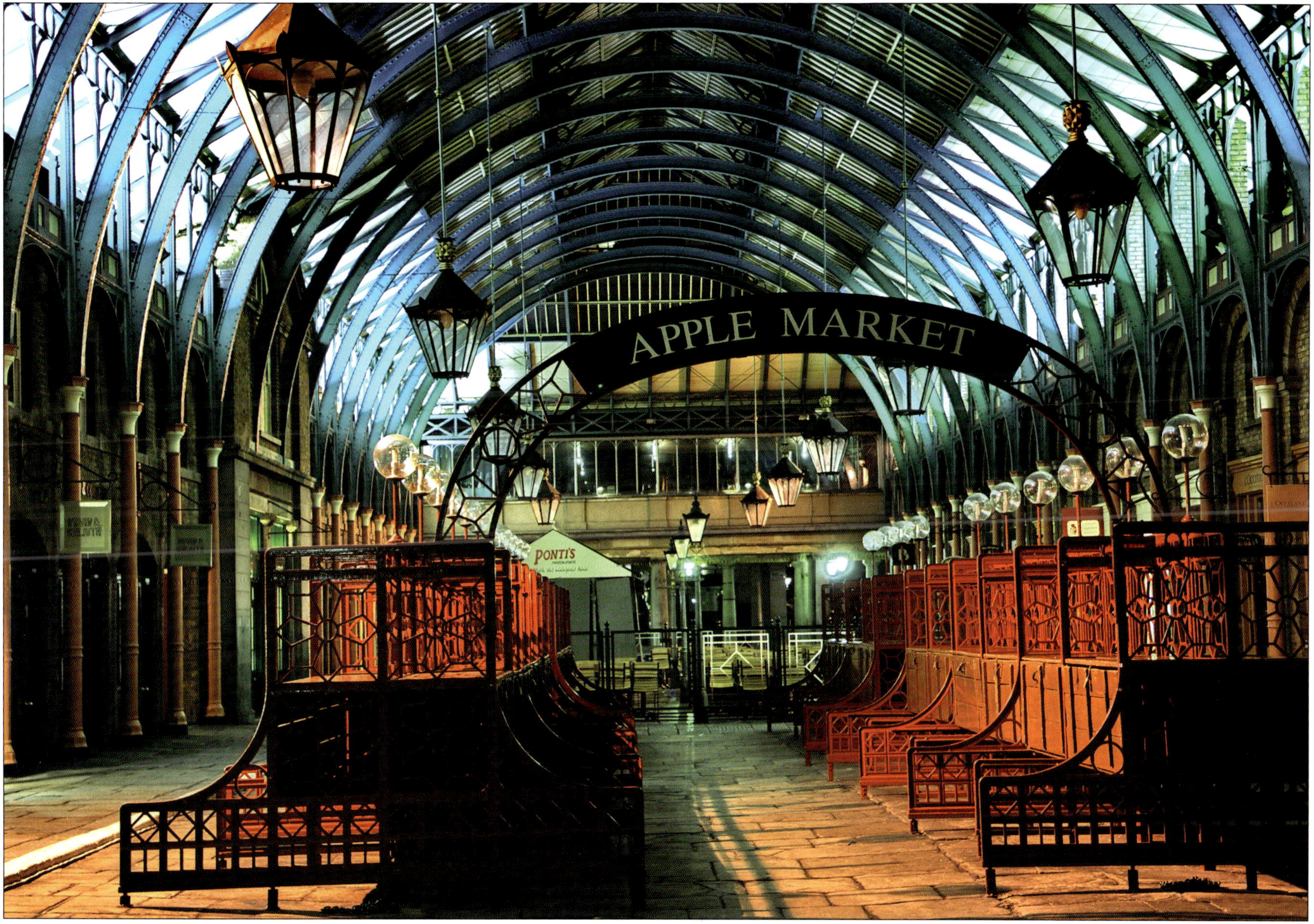

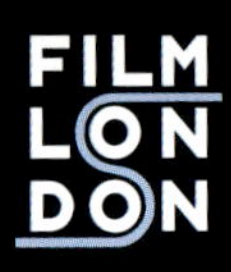

Bear Mountain, London Zoo

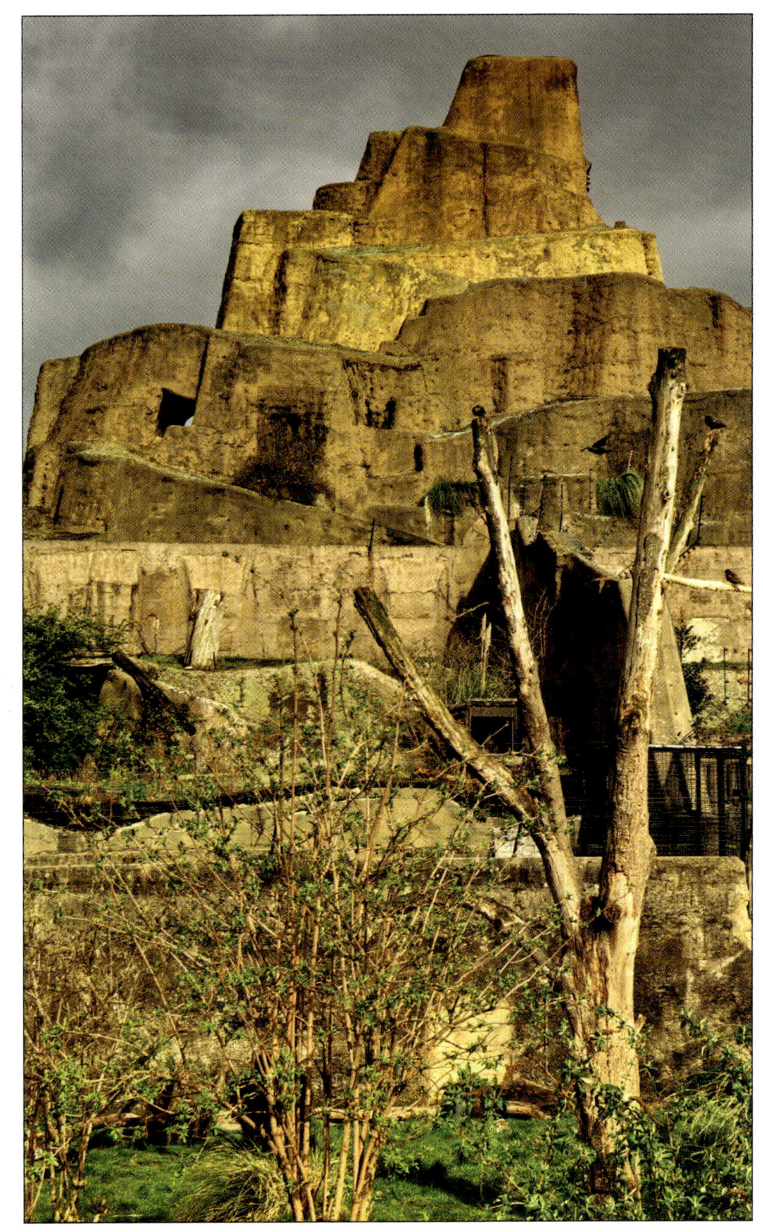

Halls of Residence, the University of East London

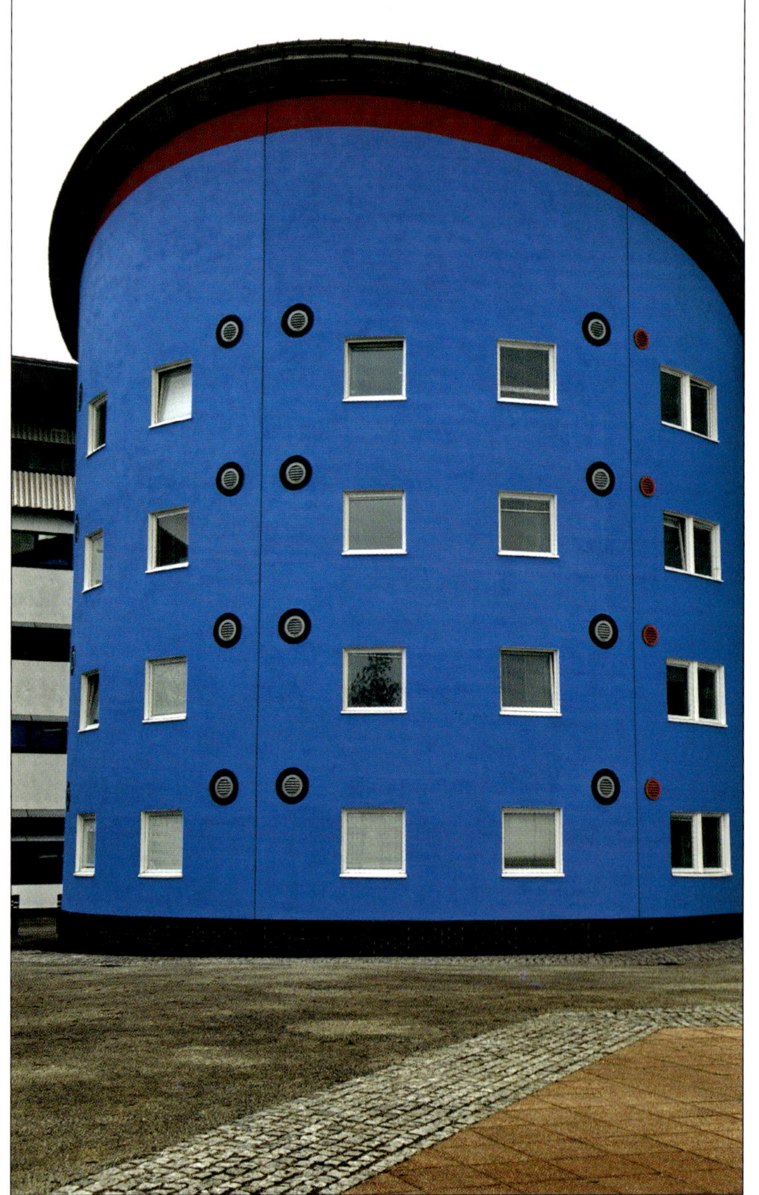

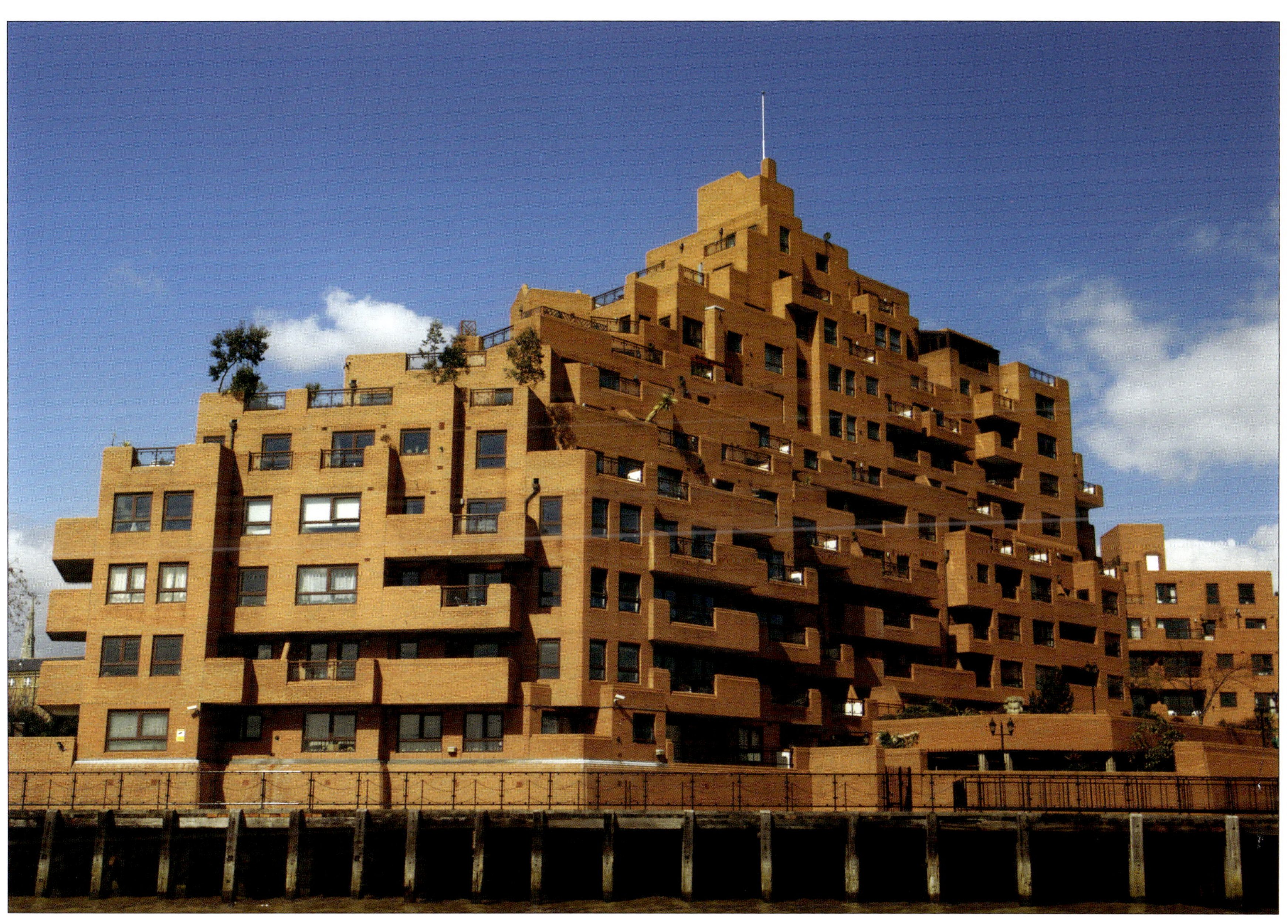

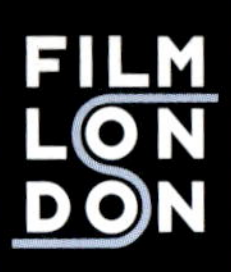

View from the Hilton Hotel, Park Lane

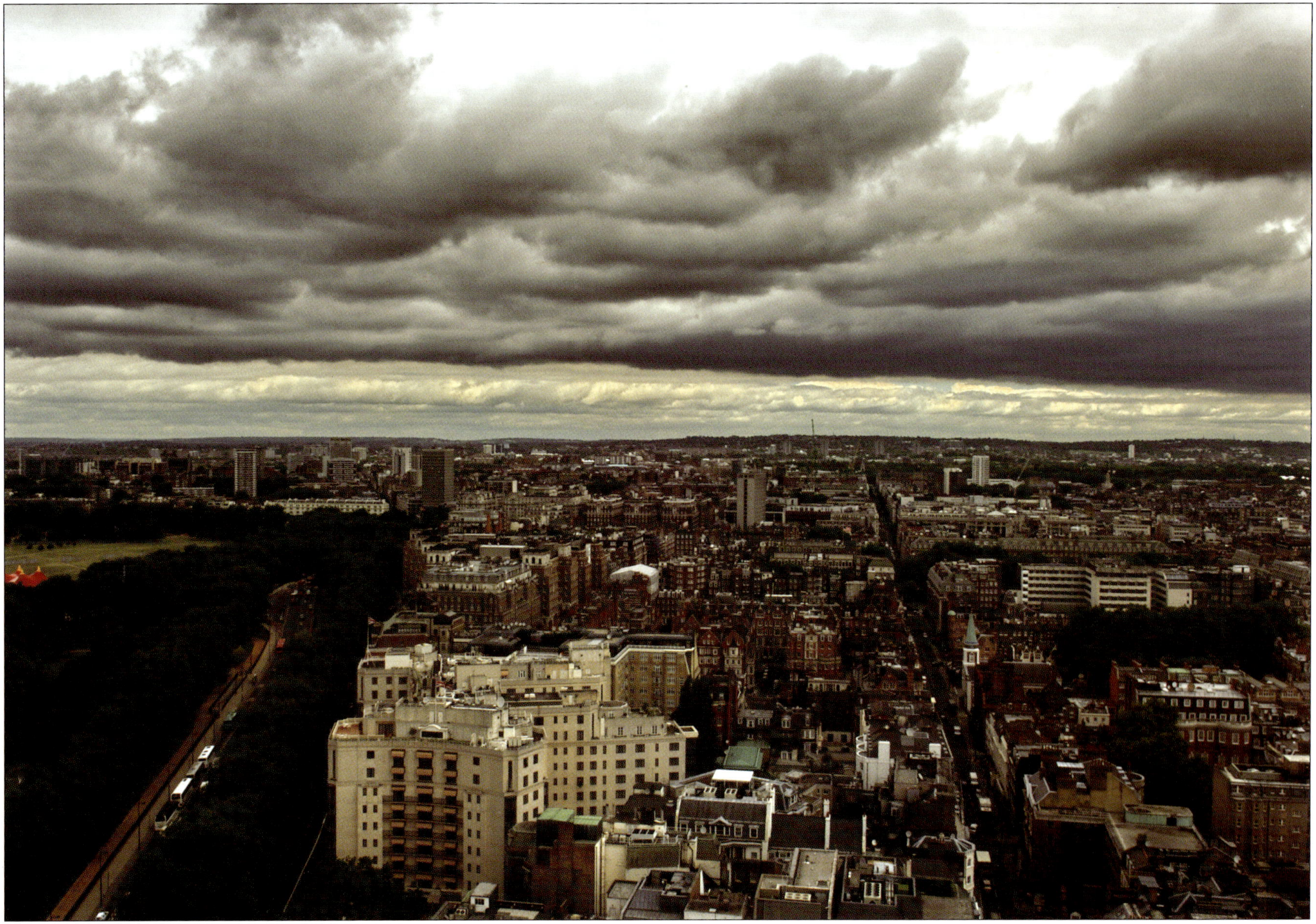

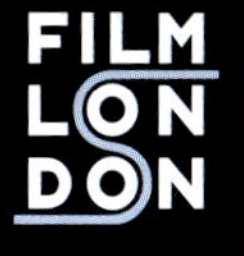

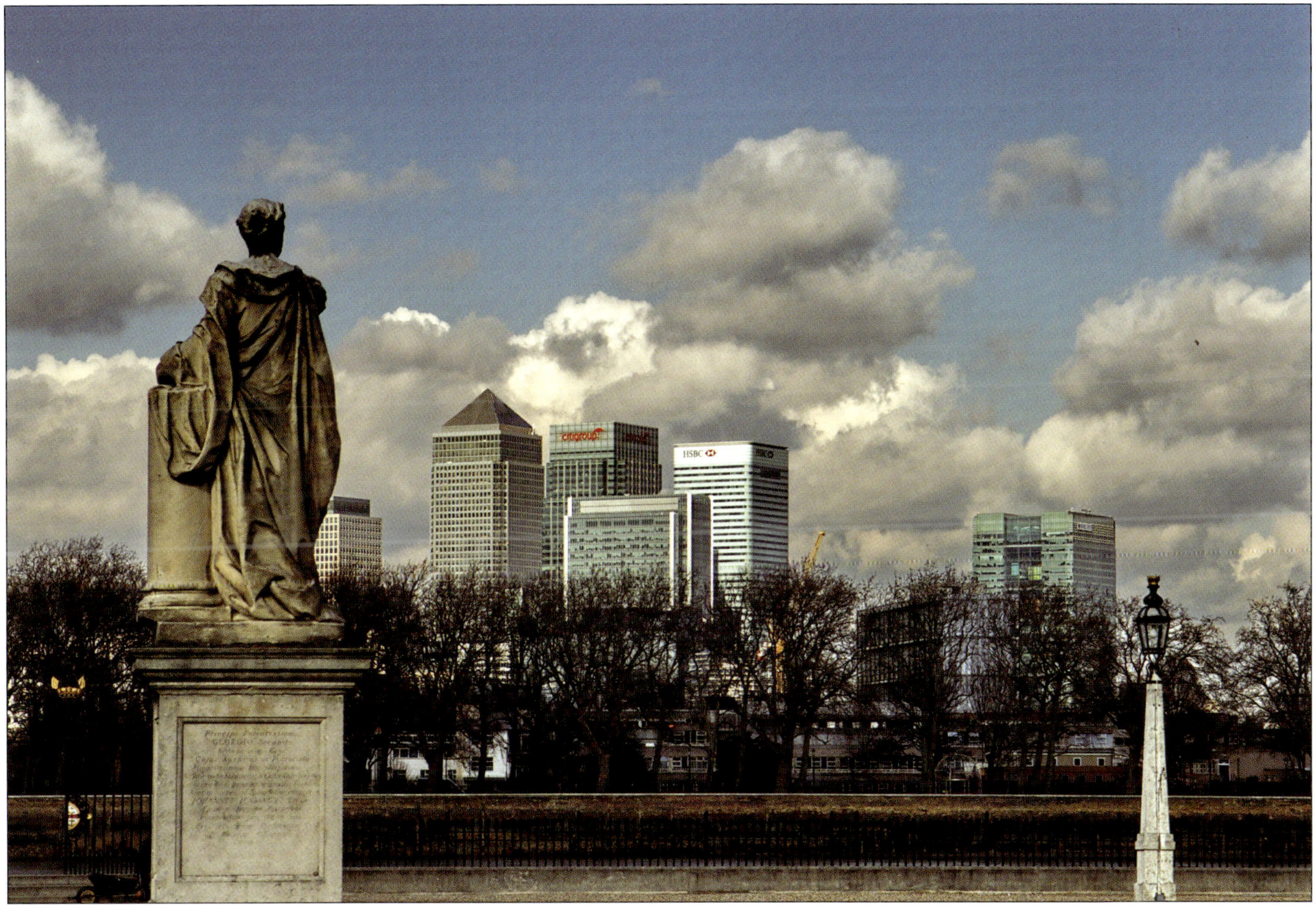

View from the Royal Naval College, Greenwich

London is a great screen, a palimpsest of past histories and of individual lives. It is haunted by the images of those who have gone before, framed by forgotten and buried buildings, and silvered by a patina of London dust. It reflects all the faces of Londoners, past and present, and in doing so creates a narrative of unbearable complexity and beauty.

Peter Ackroyd

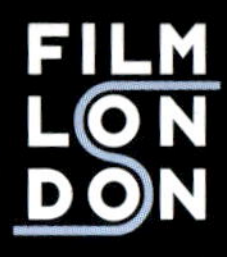
FILM
LON
DON

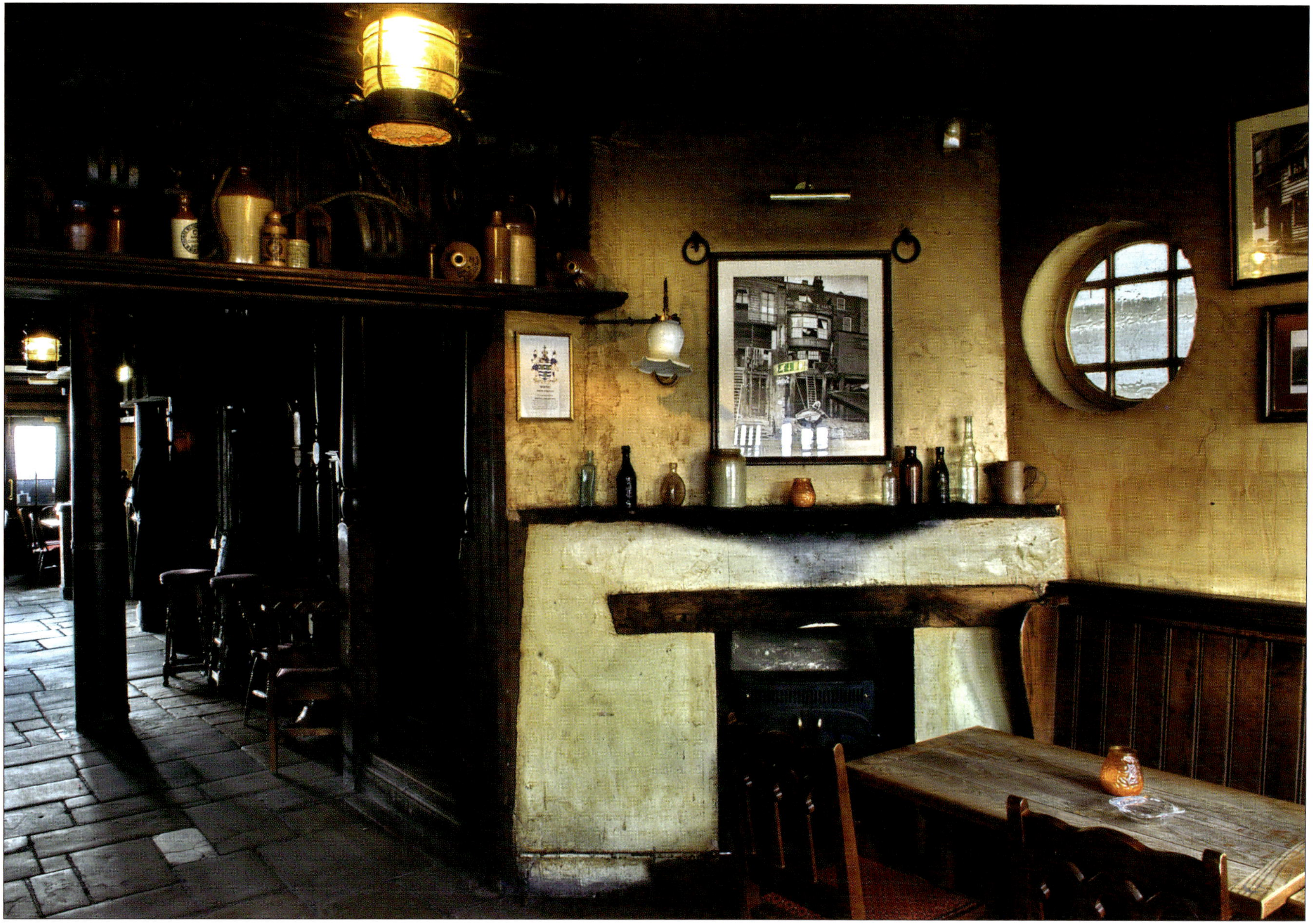

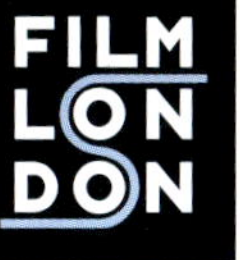
FILM
LON
DON

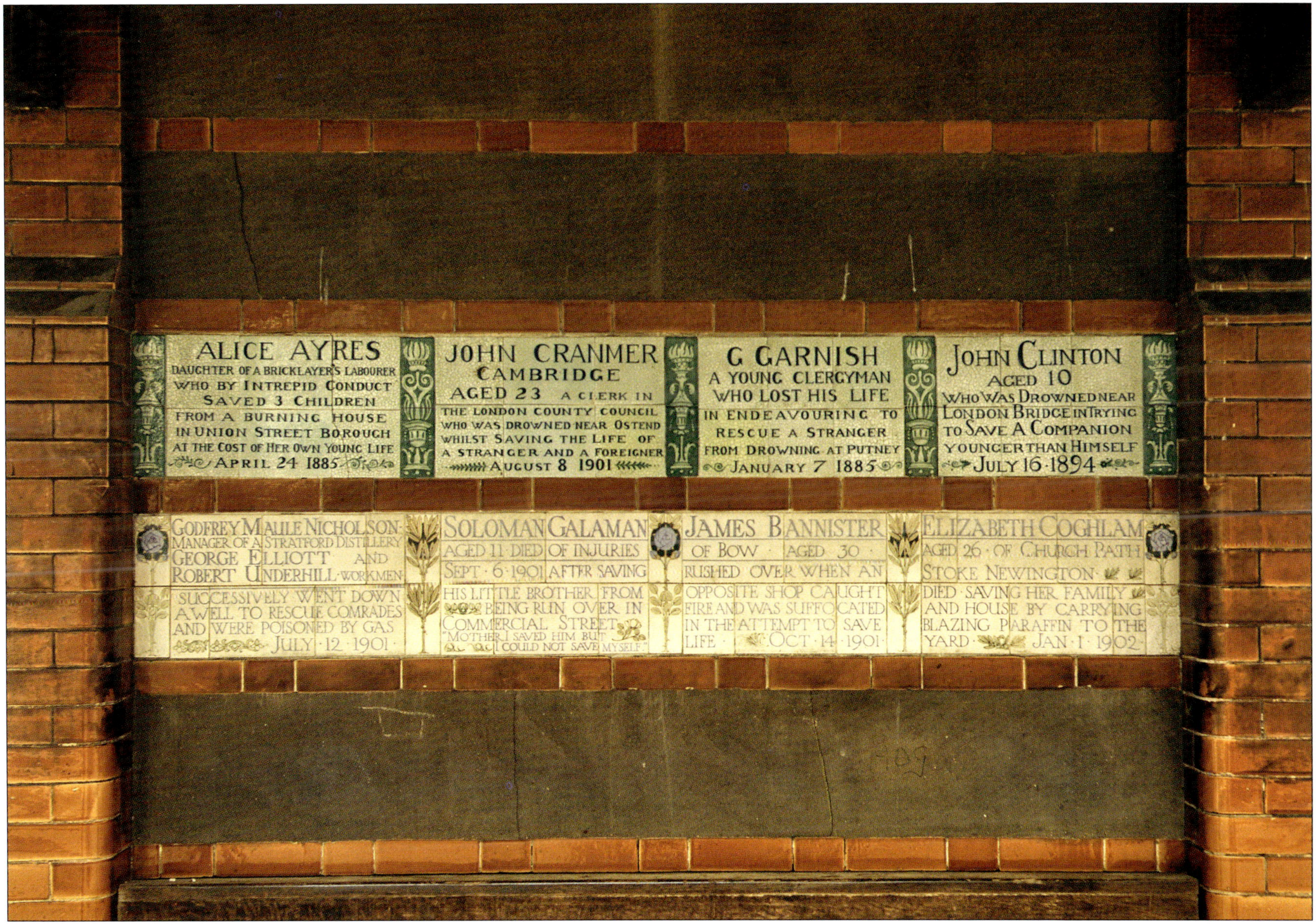

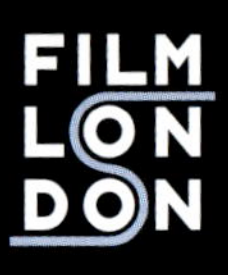
FILM
LONDON

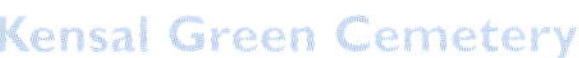

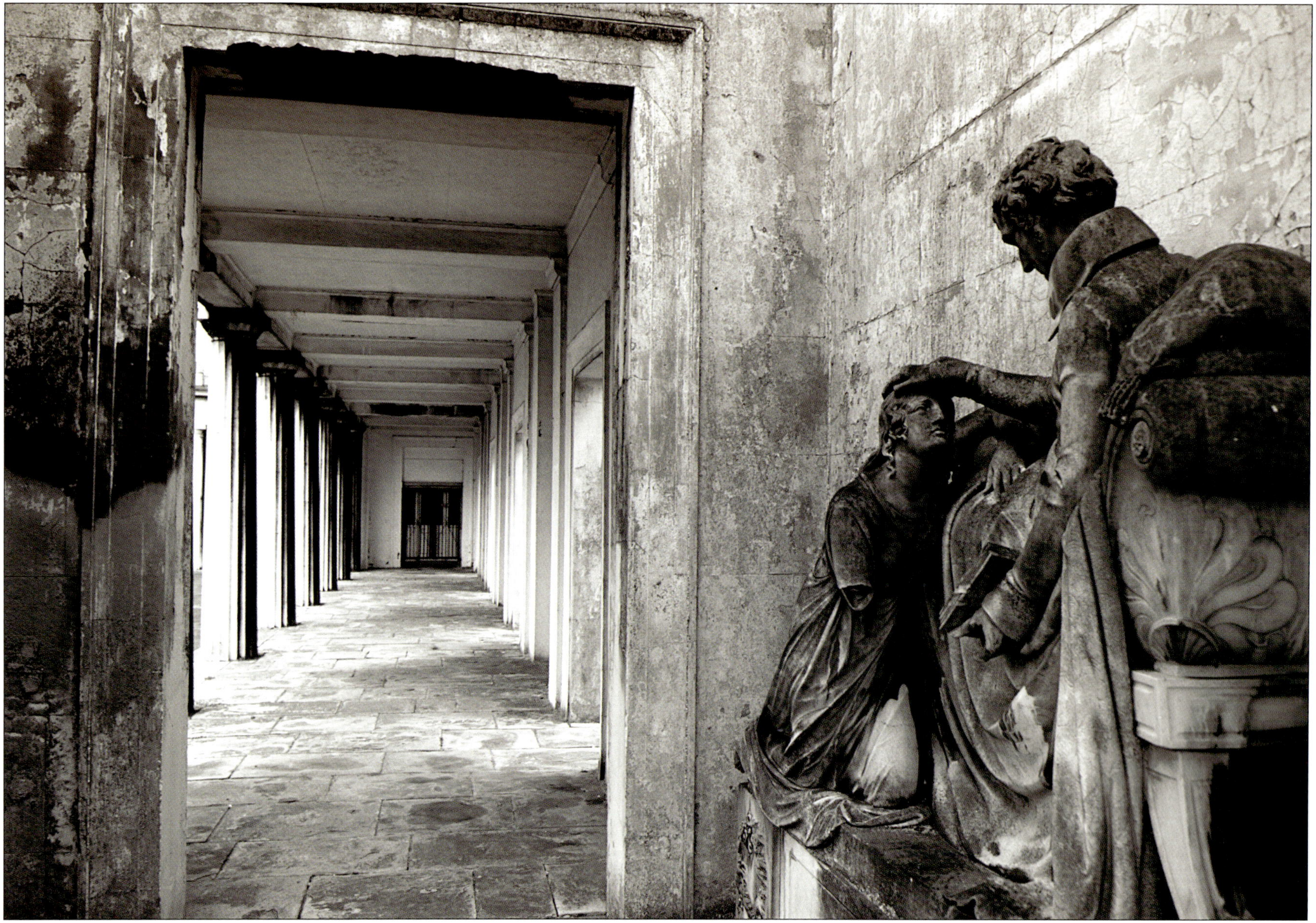

Laban, Creekside

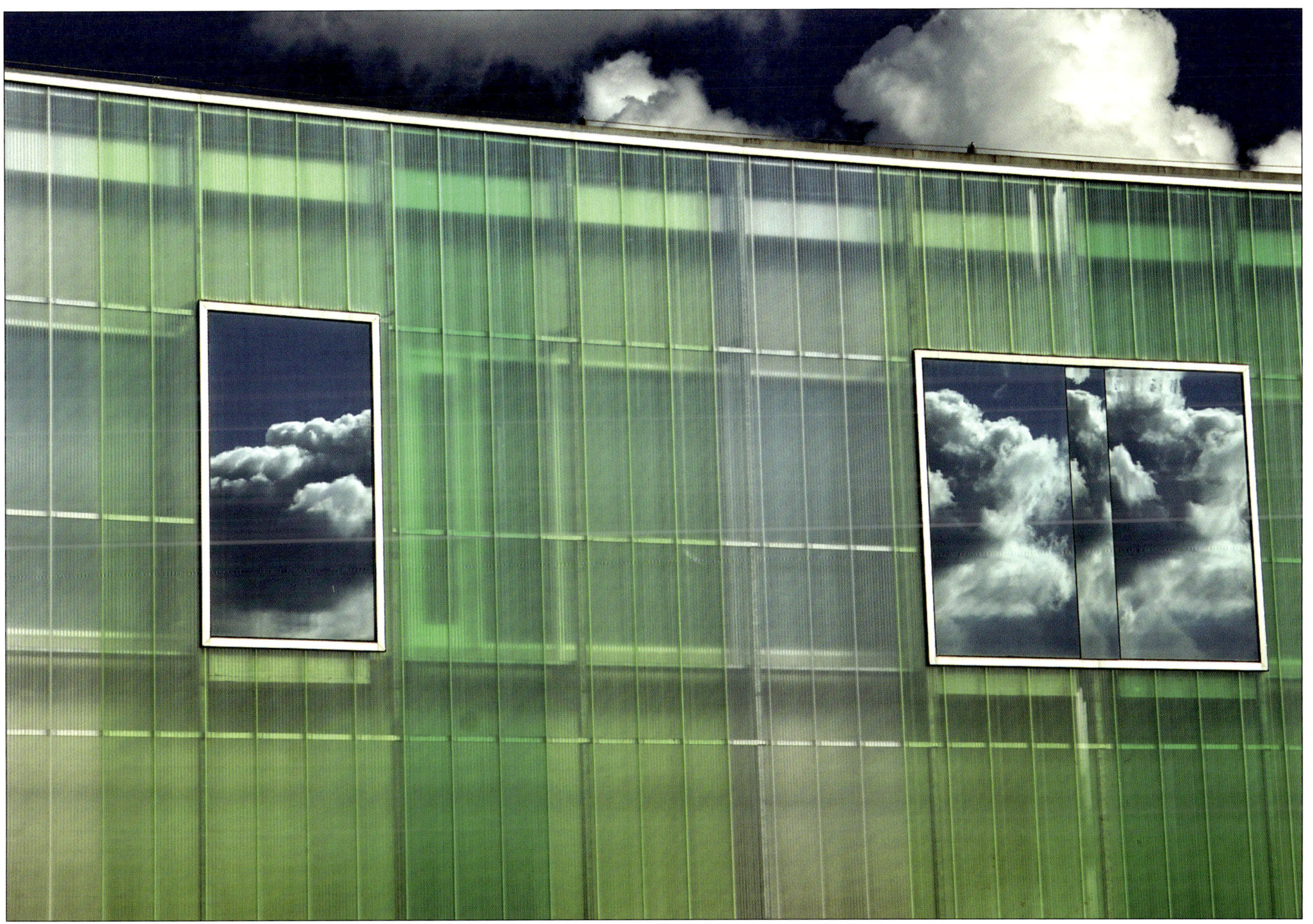

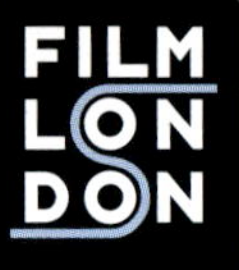

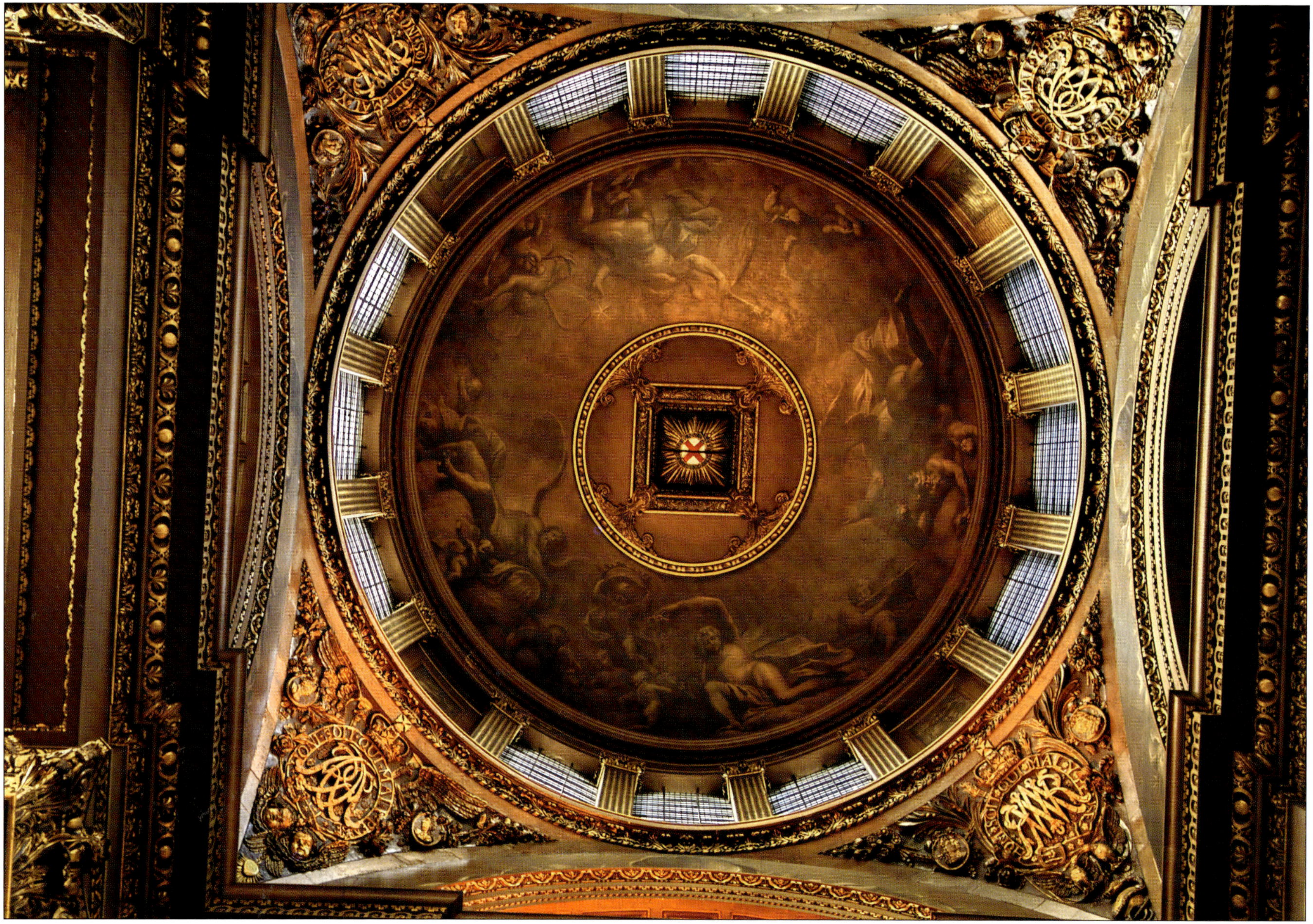

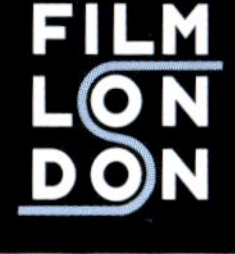

When I made a film of Joseph Conrad's *The Secret Agent*, we soon worked out that Conrad's dingy, mud-spattered late Victorian Soho (which he described as 'an immensity of greasy slime and damp plaster') would have to be recreated in the studio; what was surprising, however, was just how much remained in London (unlike New York or Paris or Berlin) that was in period, as well as being visually striking and evocative. We filmed at Woolwich Academy, the Royal Maritime Museum, the Drapers' Hall (which played the Russian Embassy's interior) and Somerset House (which played its exterior). Then there was the red-brick cathedral of St. Pancras, its platforms and the strange subterranean passageways below; and, of course, Greenwich Observatory, a central character in the story, still perched on the summit of Greenwich Park, filmable from any number of angles. In my film *Carrington*, set in the nineteen-twenties, it was also possible to find whatever we needed in London: it's so vast, layered and multifarious a city, even the most demanding film-maker will be sure to find those demands met, if not exceeded.

Christopher Hampton

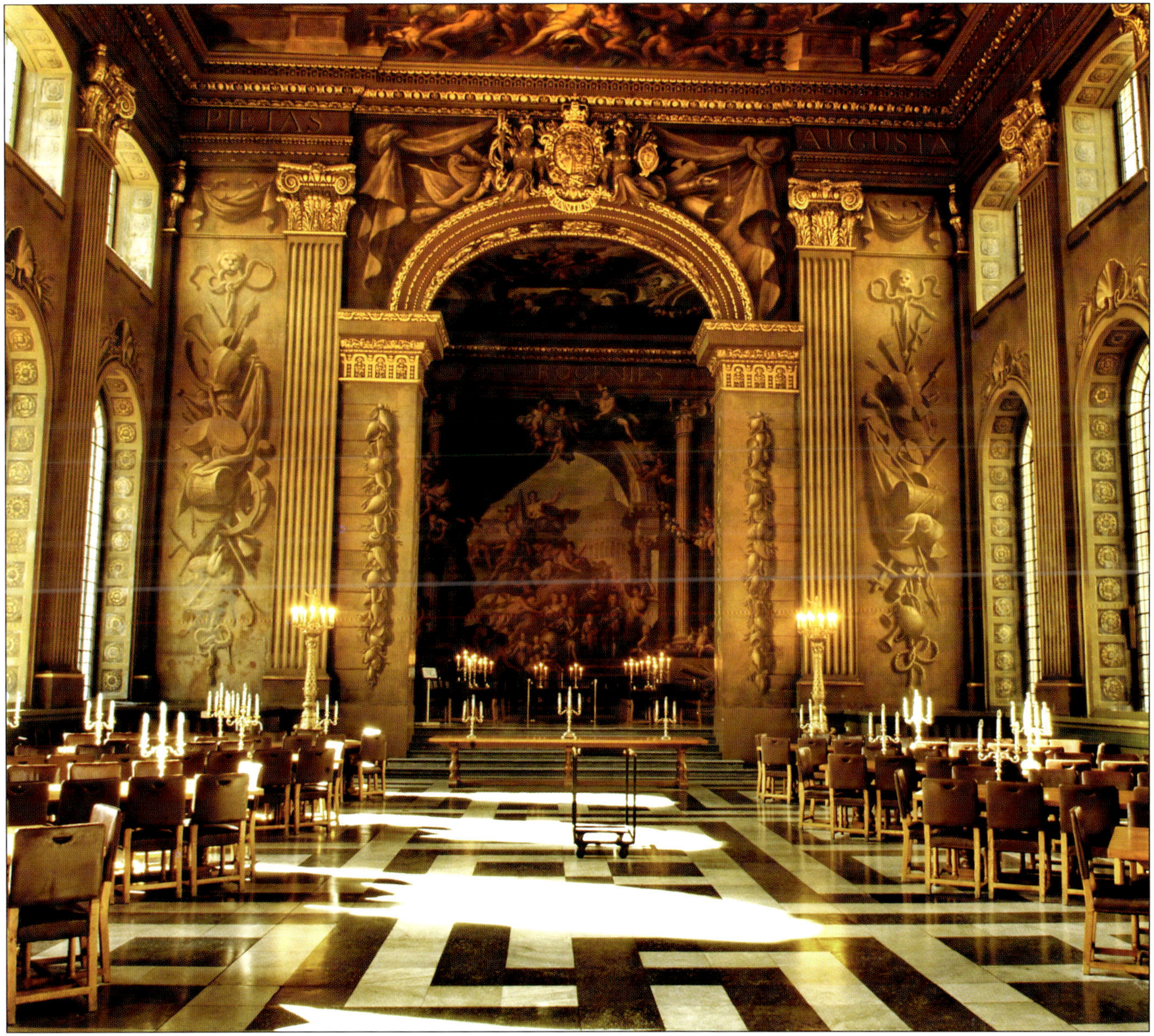

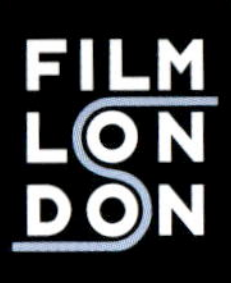

BaySixty6 Skatepark, Kensington & Chelsea

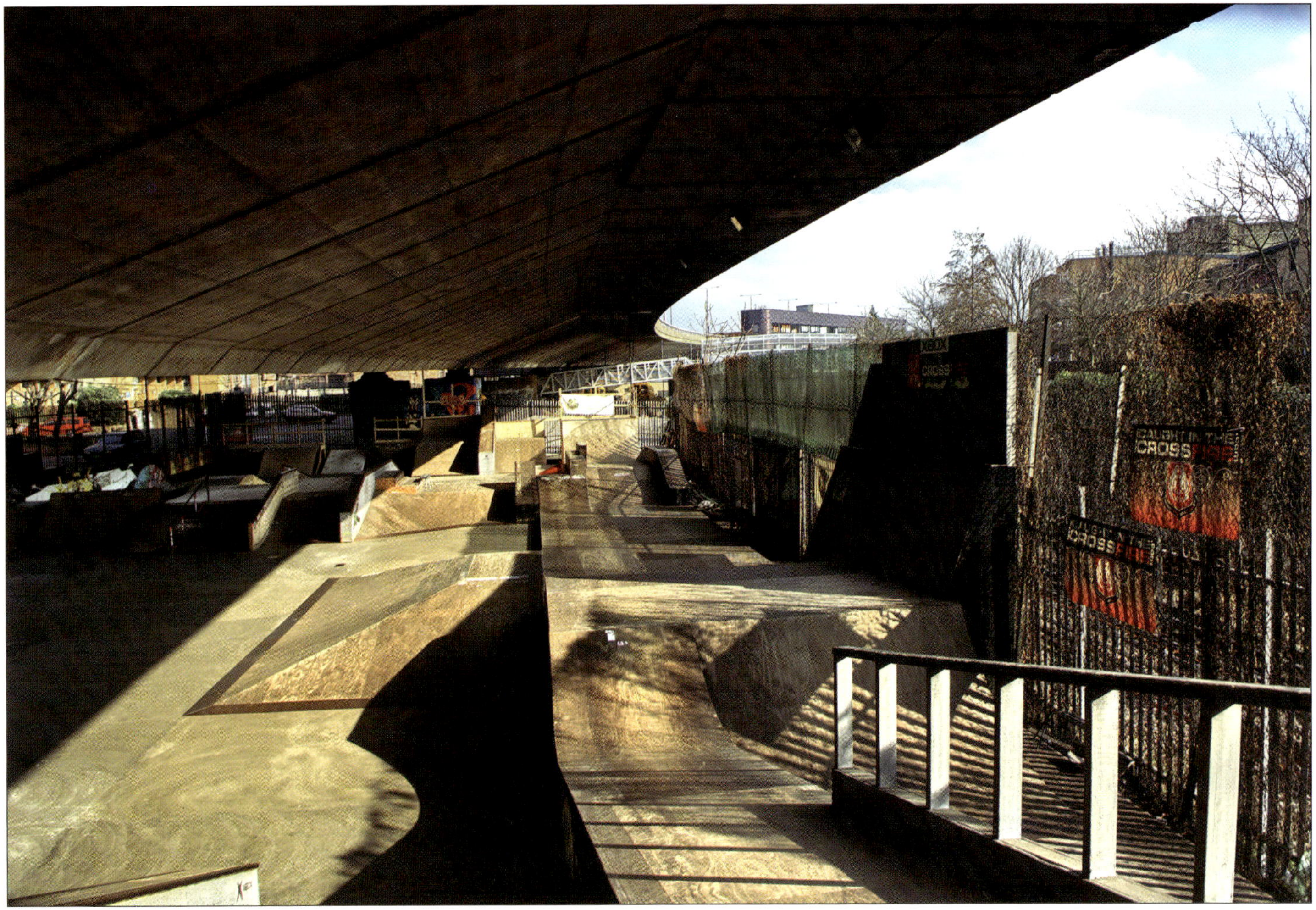

London has everything, good and bad, rough and smooth, sweet and sour. There's 360 degrees of history, progress, decay, ruin and splendour to photograph, to inflect a scene. There really is a story on every corner. London offers almost pastoral views, then clotted, industrial ones; its variety is breathtaking, its eccentric street map, its nooks and crannies. The river runs through it, and the canals with their own secret lives and atmospheres. And the best of London is this diversity, not only in geography but in people, in faces, in experience. (A Kosovan community in the middle of West Hampstead, a Portuguese one in Notting Hill). If you're tired of shooting in London, you're tired of shooting life.

Anthony Minghella

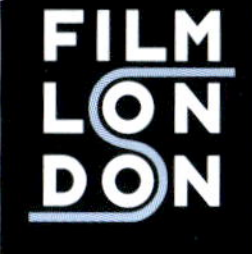
FILM
LON
DON

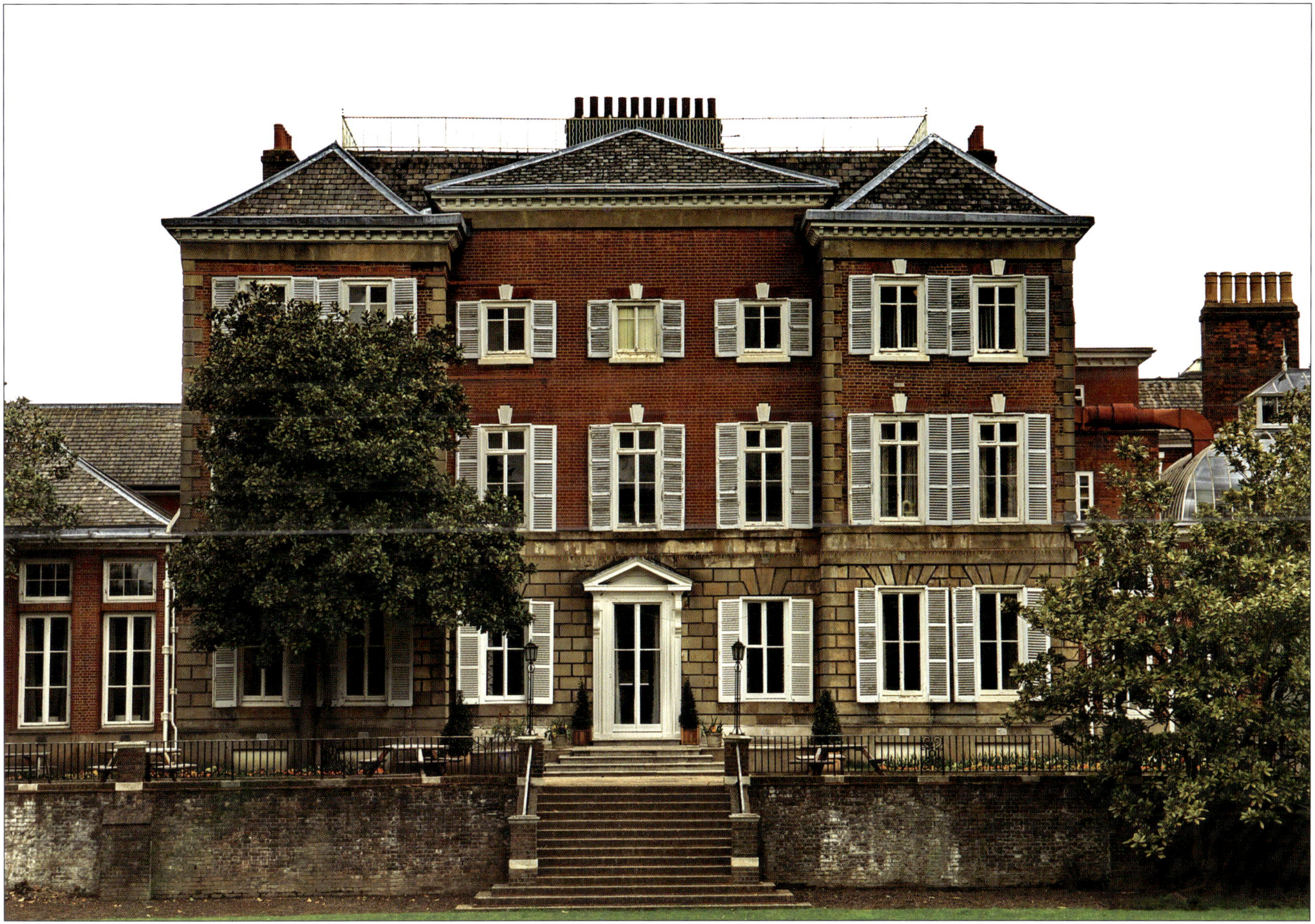

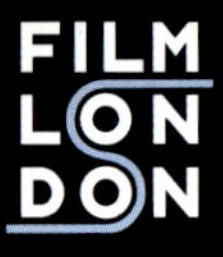

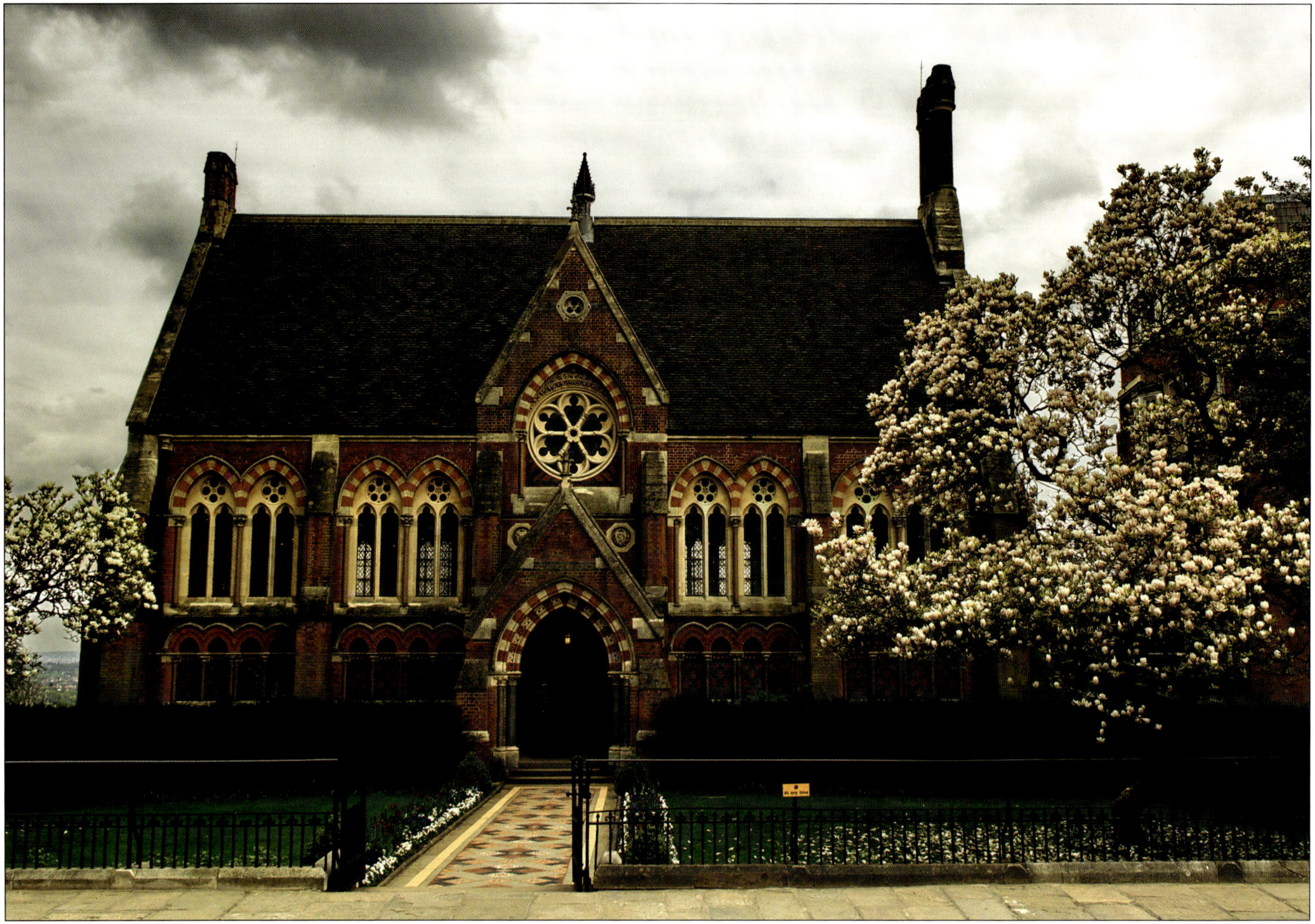

The Vaughan Library, Harrow School

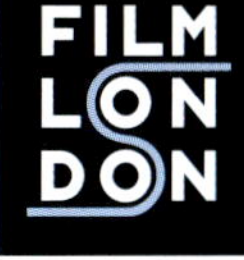
FILM
LONDON

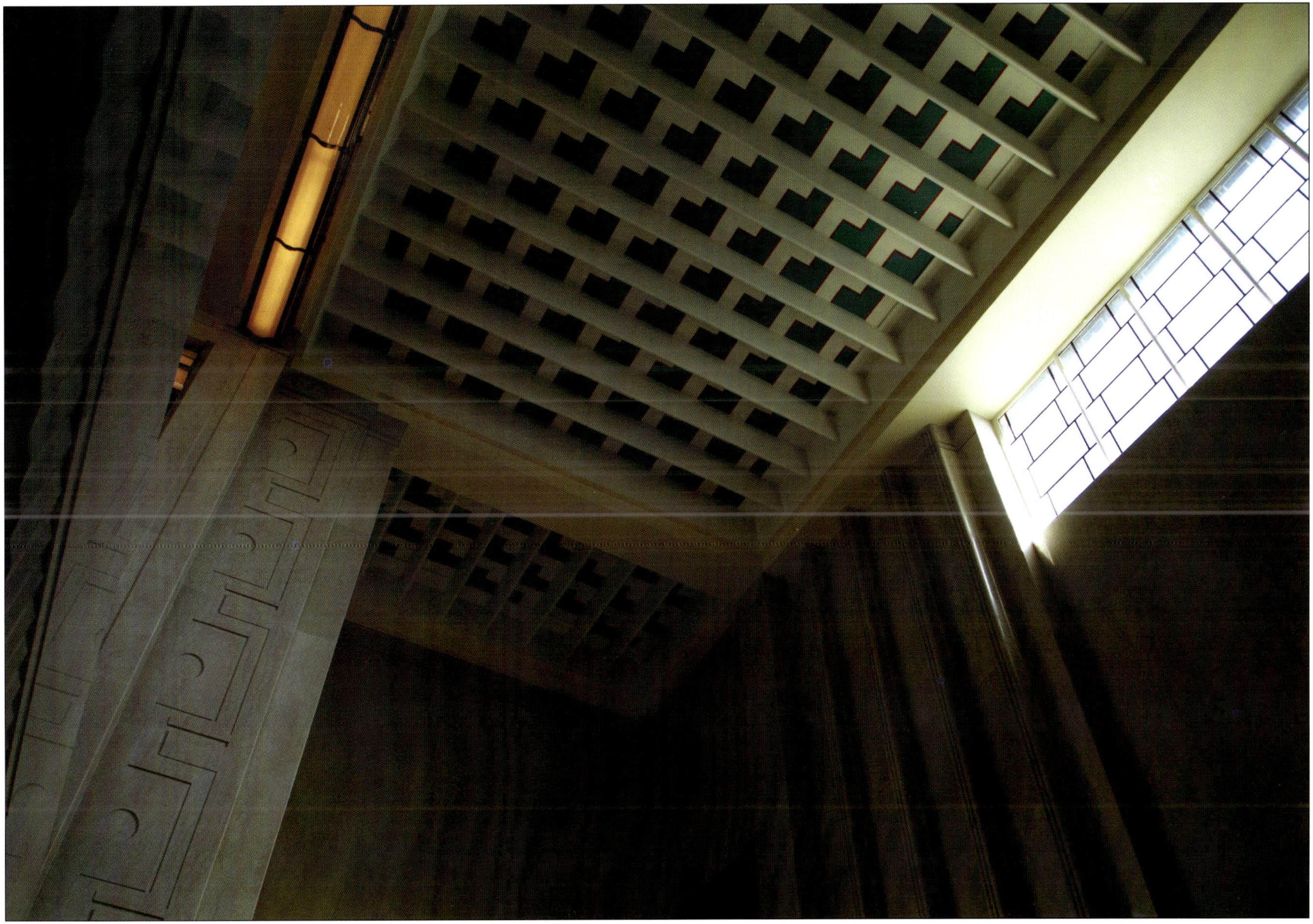

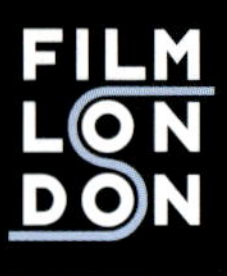

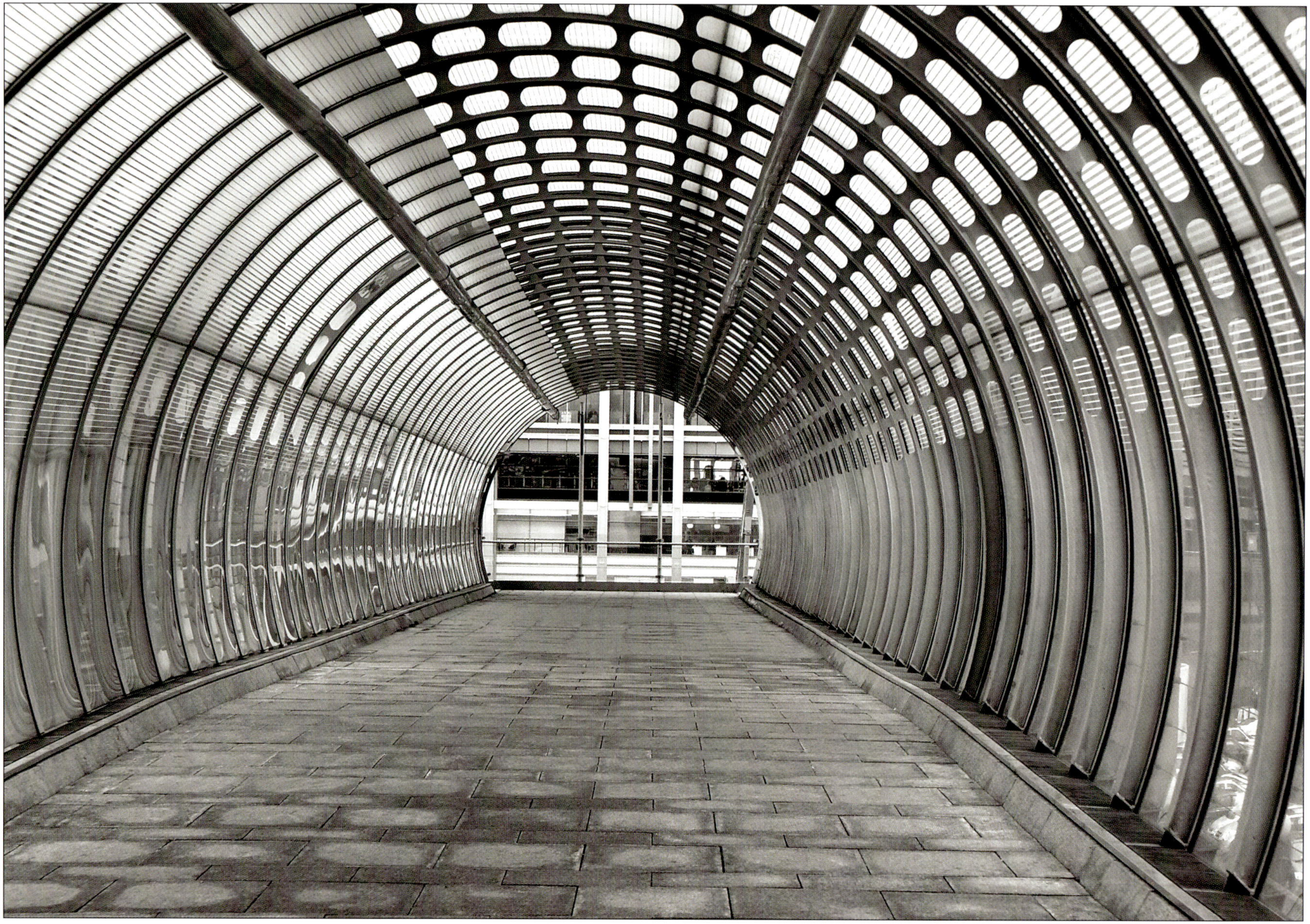

Footbridge, Poplar DLR Station

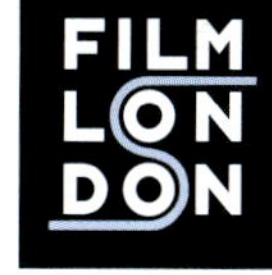
FILM
LONDON

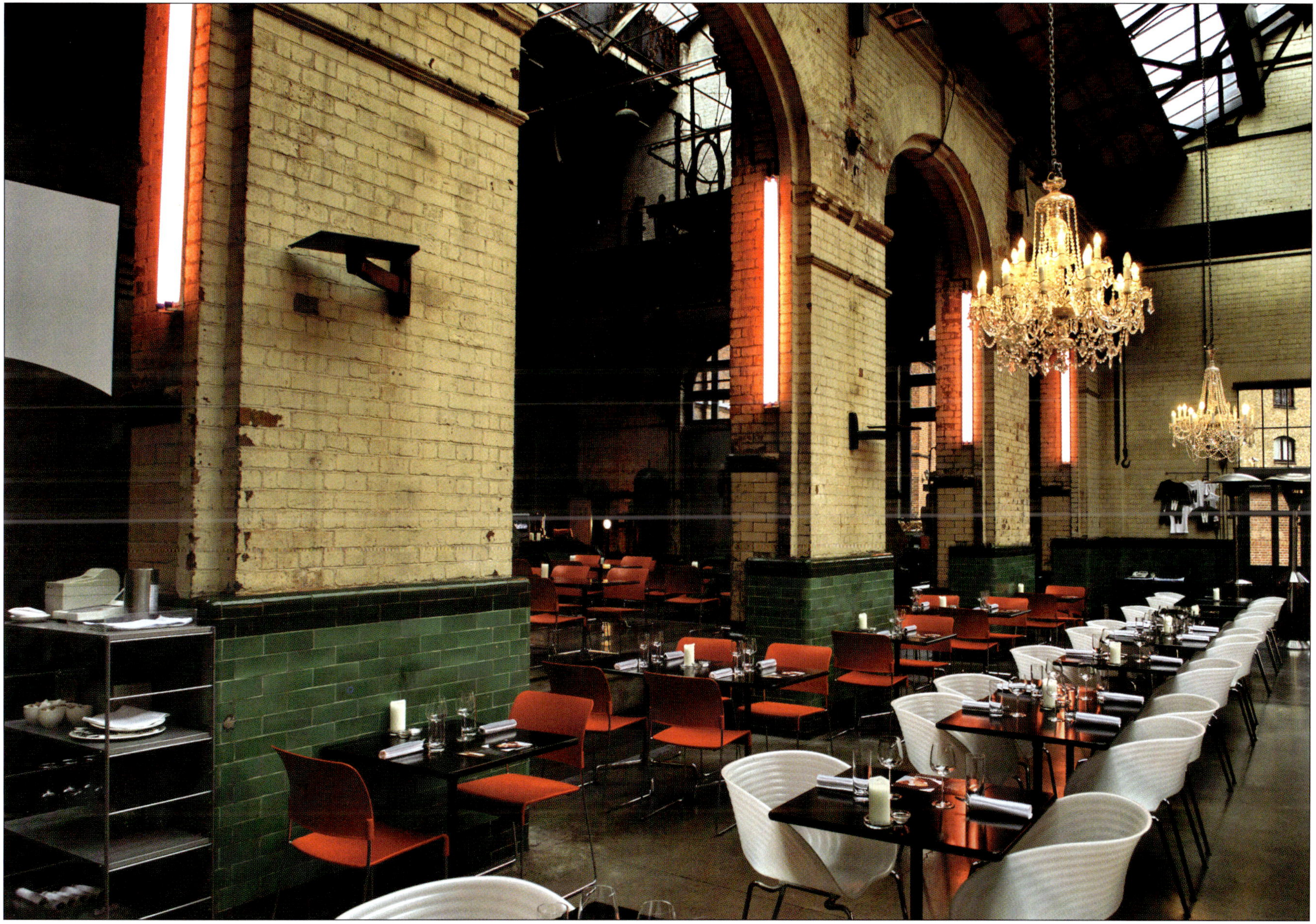

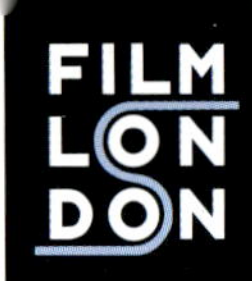
FILM
LON
DON

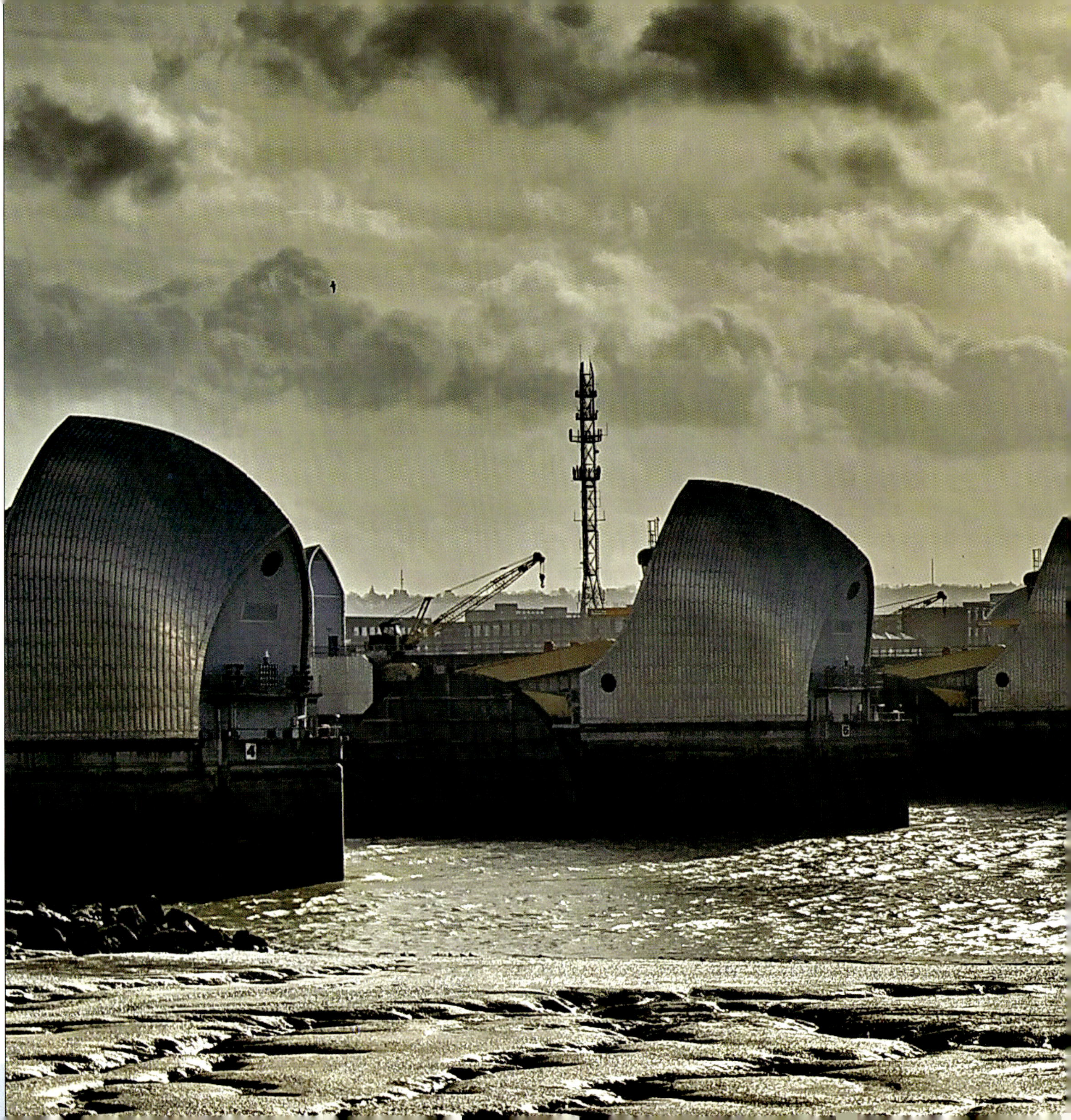

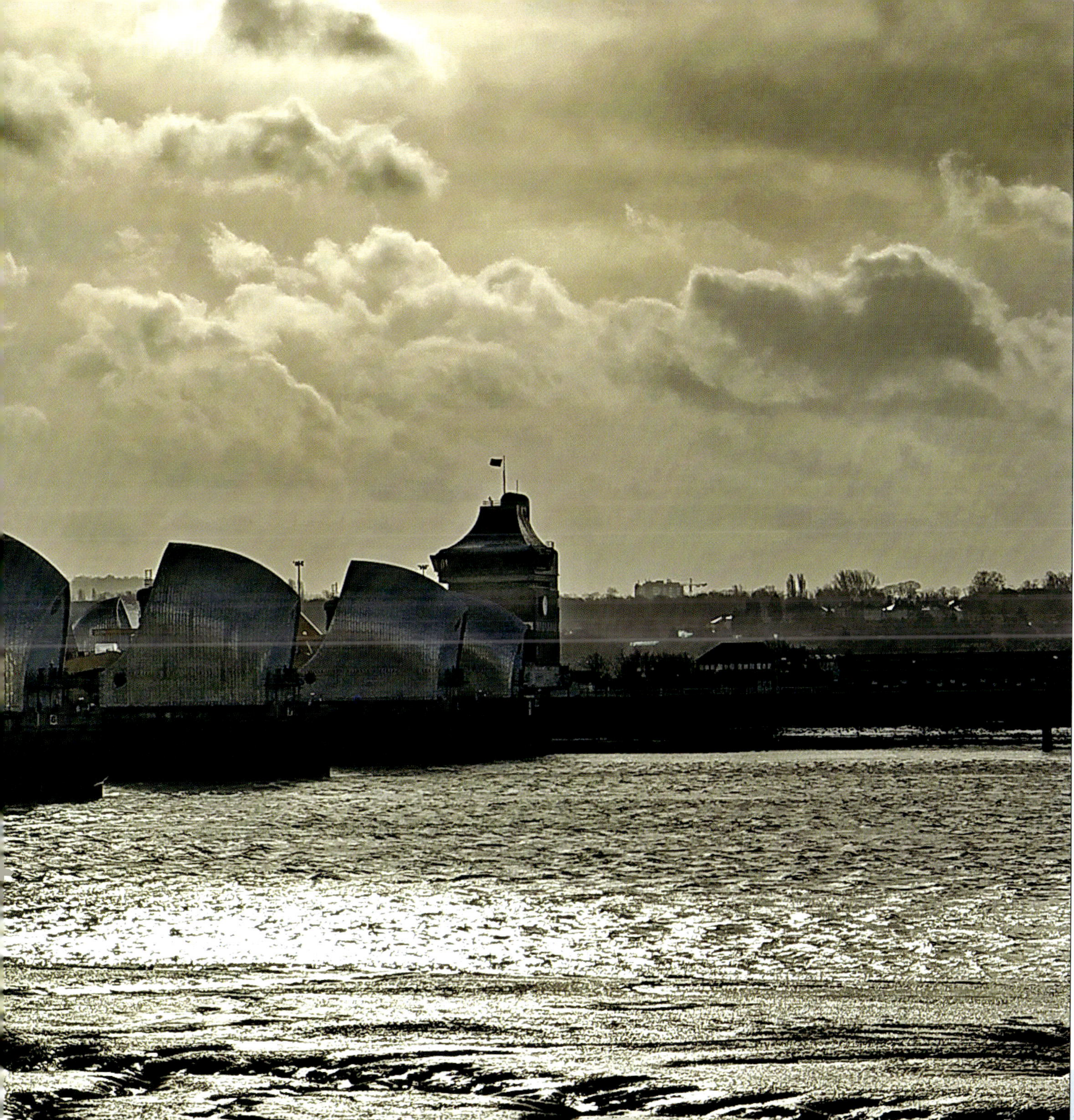

Landscapes inspire me to tell stories and I'm interested in the link between them and human emotions.

Juliet McKoen

Turbine Hall, Tate Modern

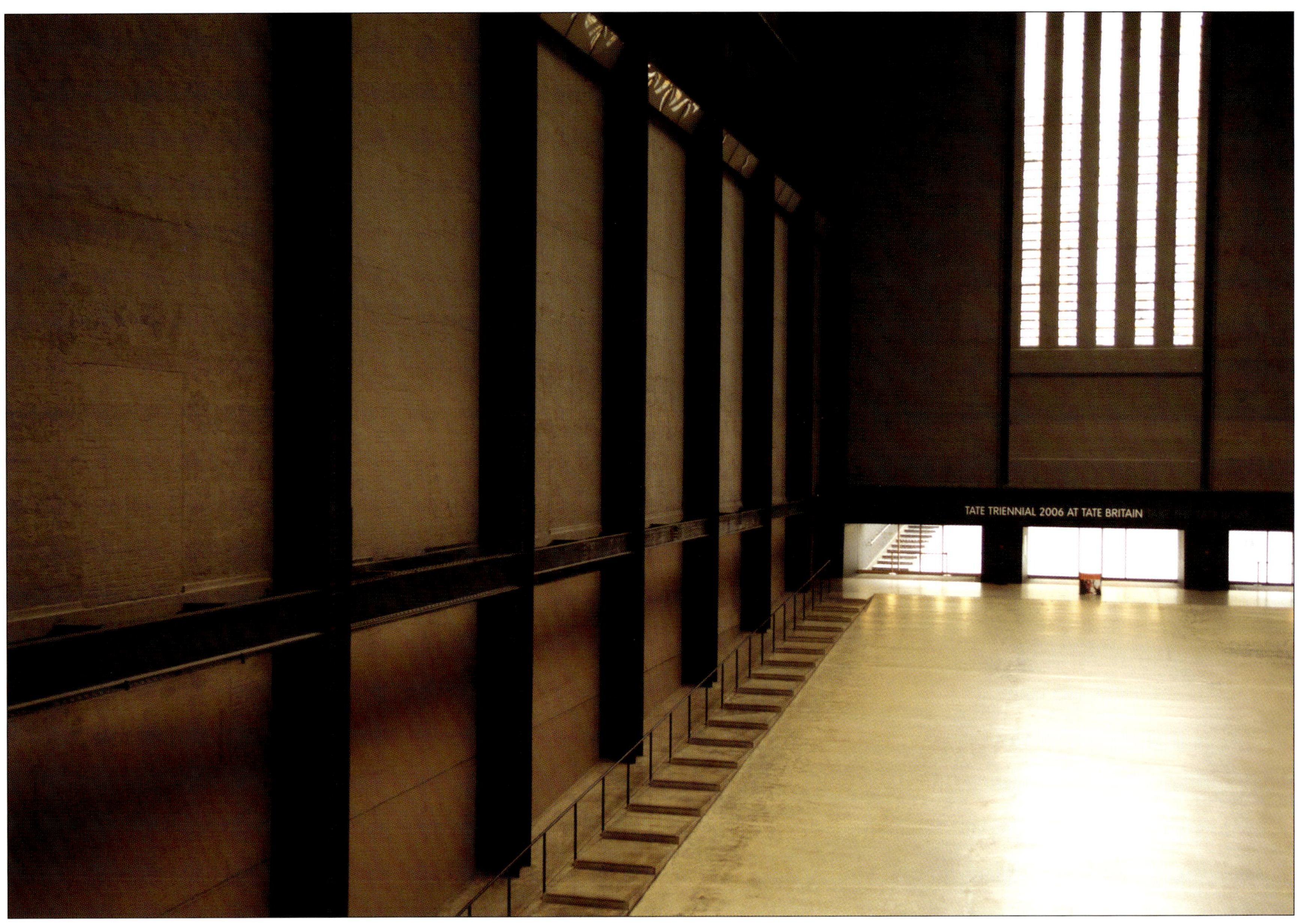

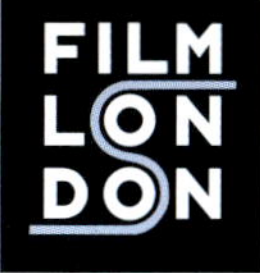

The Windmill Theatre at dawn

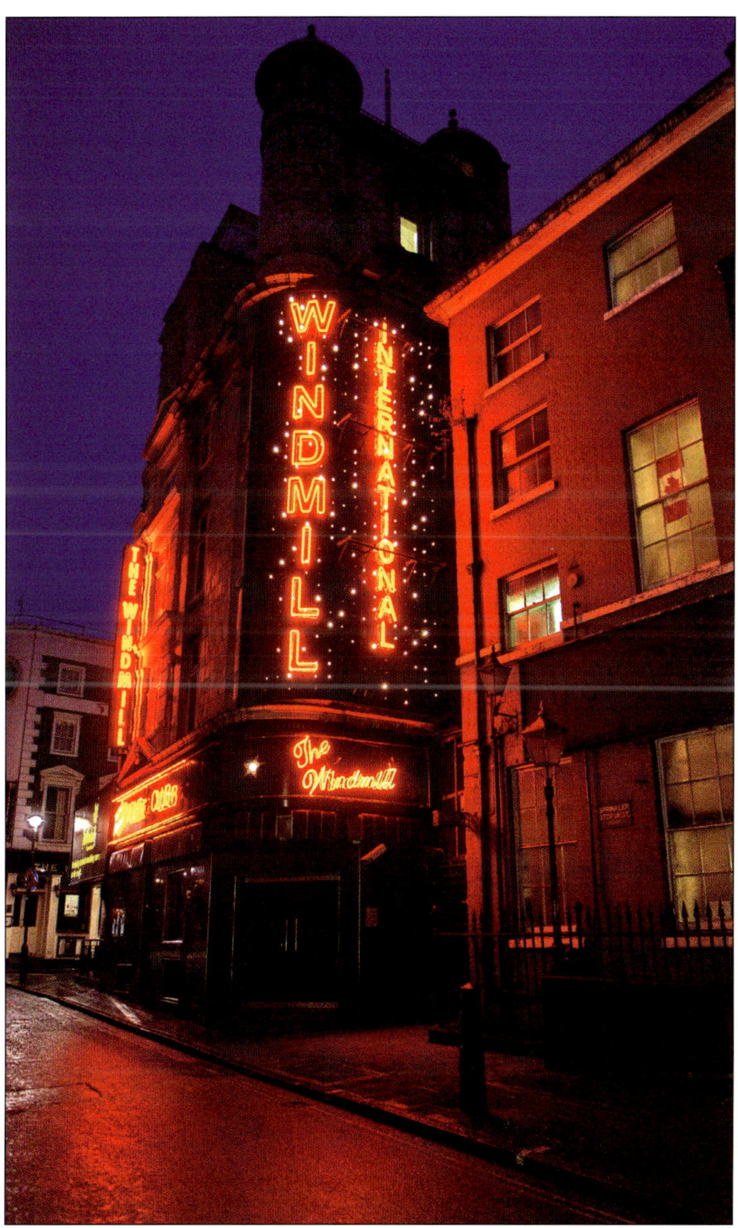

London is having a wonderful moment, and one which might well continue indefinitely. It's better than the so-called swinging 60s - now, the architecture, the music, the movies, the art scene - all are vibrantly celebrating a community that moves with and mirrors the world at large. No other city is so redolent of the past and so embracing of the future: it's the best city in the world to live in, and it contains more stories than we can imagine. What Roger Michell and I have tried to do in our last three films is to show, alongside the beautiful re-discoveries and transformations of this ancient site, the city we live in - local, sometimes scruffy, but always fascinating.

Kevin Loader

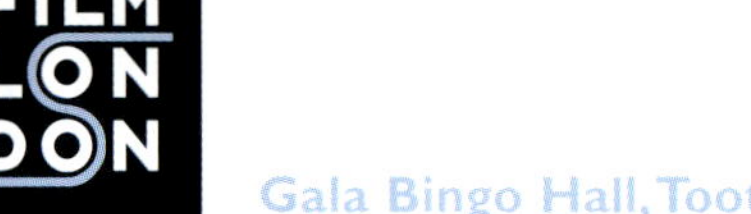

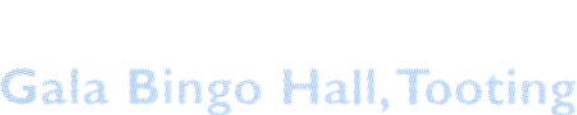

Gala Bingo Hall, Tooting

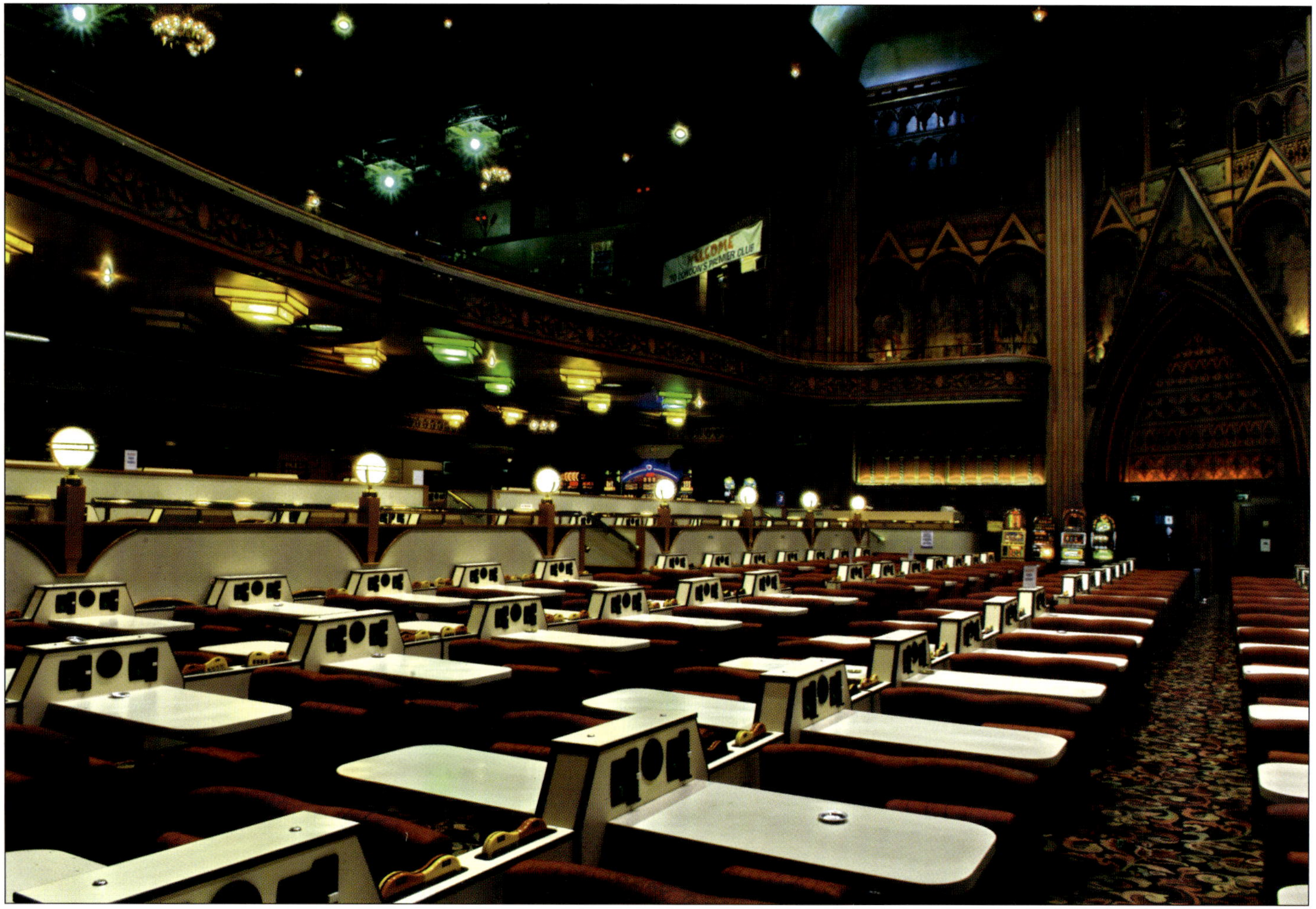

London is a city with so many cities within, a city where more languages are spoken than I even knew existed, a city where every visitor from anywhere can find a corner that reflects their part of the world - kept alive by London's thriving, diverse population. London is my life blood and provides a perfect backdrop to the worlds I like to create. Whether I shoot in London or not, its essence is always reflected in my work.

Gurinder Chadha

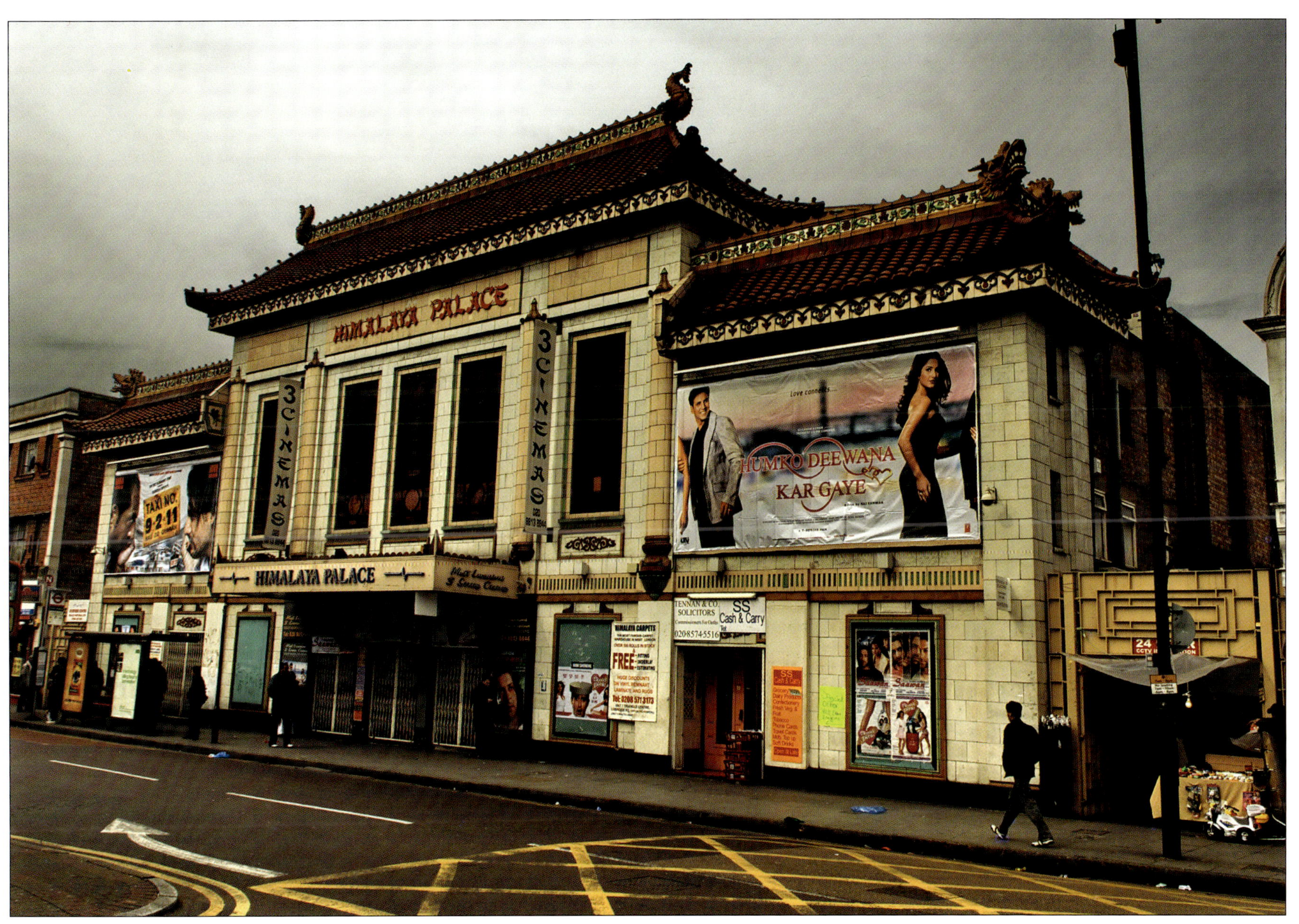
HIMALAYA PALACE
3 CINEMAS
HUMKO DEEWANA KAR GAYE
TAXI NO. 9 2 11
TENNAN & CO. SOLICITORS
SS Cash & Carry
FREE

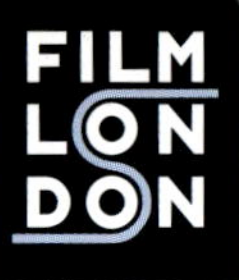

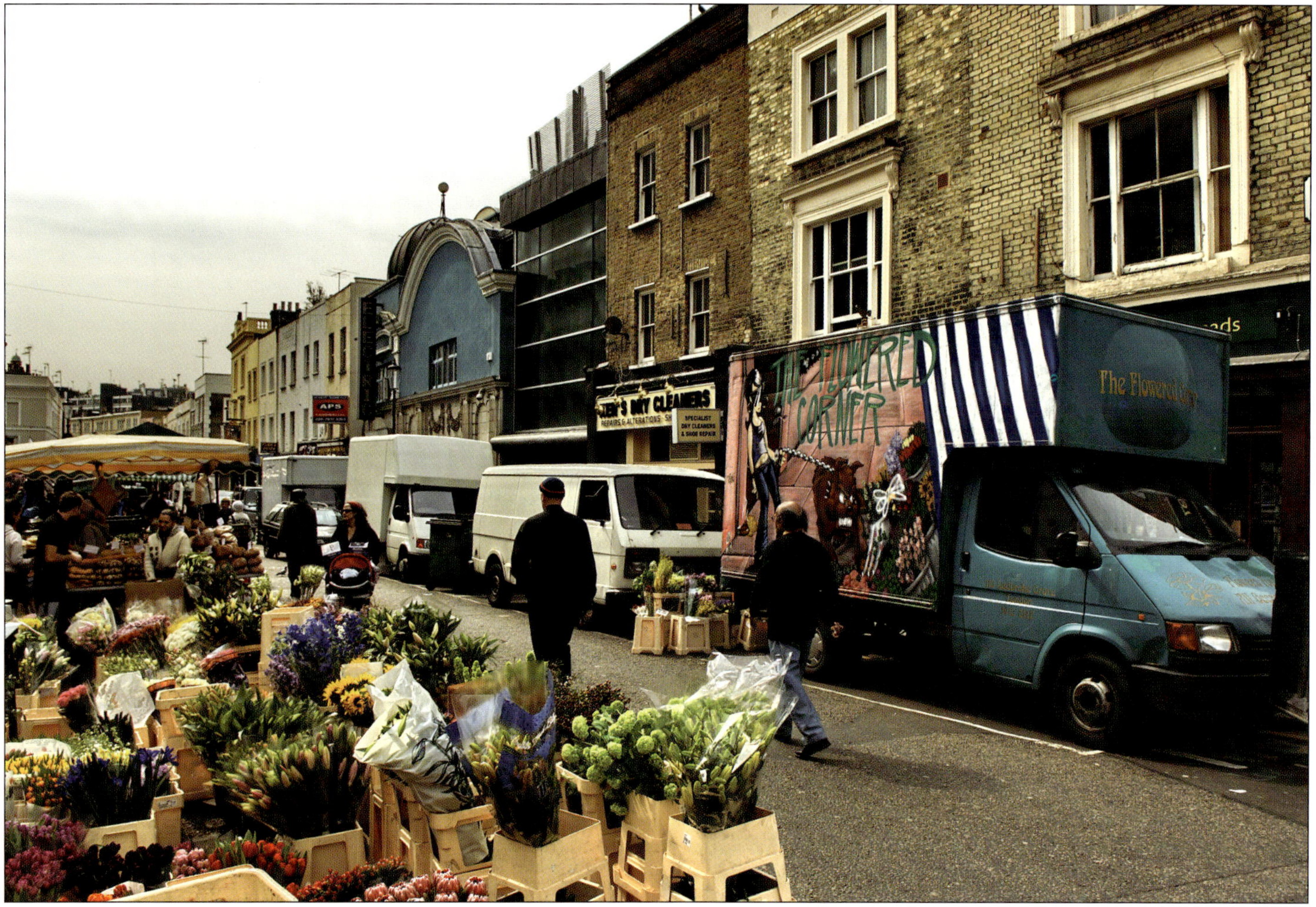

It always seems to me that the star of the film is London.

Richard Curtis

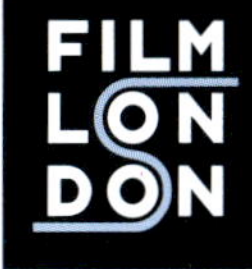

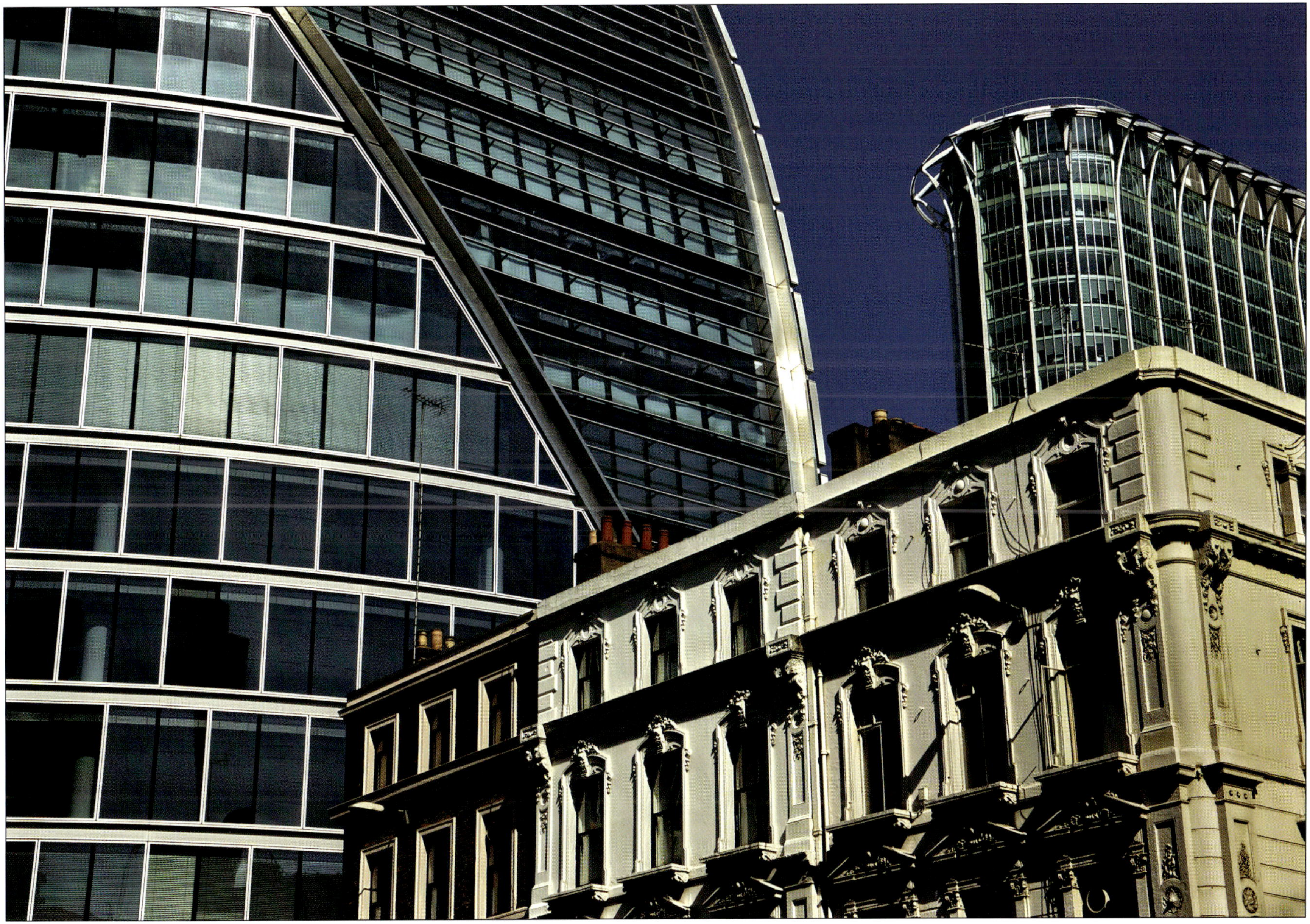

Moorgate, City of London

30 St Mary Axe. Credits include: *Basic Instinct II; Match Point*
Abbey Mills Pumping Station - Locality Unlimited. Credits include: *Batman Begins; Thunderbirds*
Barking & Dagenham Civic Centre. Credits include: *Hustle*
BaySixty6 Skatepark, Kensington & Chelsea. Credits include: *Sammy & Rosie Get Laid*
Covent Garden. Credits include: *Frenzy*
Gala Bingo Hall, Tooting - The Gala Coral Croup.
Hammersmith Bridge. Credits include: *Waking the Dead; Sliding Doors; Martha, Meet Frank, Daniel and Laurence*
Harrow School. Credits include: *Harry Potter and the Philosopher's Stone; The Saint; Pride & Prejudice*
Hilton Hotel, Park Lane. Credits include: *Strumpet*
Kensal Green Cemetery. Credits include: *The Fourth Angel; The End of the Affair; Look Back in Anger*
King's Cross Station - Network Rail. Credits include: *Harry Potter and the Goblet of Fire; Harry Potter and the Prisoner of Azkaban; Harry Potter and the Chamber of Secrets; Harry Potter and the Philosopher's Stone*
Laban, Creekside - www.laban.org
London Zoo. Credits include: *Wimbledon; About a Boy; Harry Potter and the Philosopher's Stone; Withnail & I; An American Werewolf in London*
Moorgate, City of London. Credits include: *Gangster No. 1*
Osterley Park, Hounslow - National Trust. Credits include: *Amazing Grace; Mansfield Park; Kabhi Kushi Kahbie Gham; Mrs Brown*
Piccadilly Circus, rooftop view - www.space2online.com Credits include: *Stormbreaker; Wimbledon; Bridget Jones's Diary; Agent Cody Banks 2*
Poplar DLR Station - DLR Serco. Credits include: *Goodbye Charlie Bright*
Portobello Road Market, Kensington & Chelsea. Credits include: *Notting Hill*
Postman's Park, City of London. Credits include: *Closer*
Princelet Street, Tower Hamlets. Credits include: *Shiner; Madame Bovary*
Somerset House - Somerset House Trust. Credits include: *Flyboys; Bride & Prejudice; Love Actually; Sleepy Hollow; GoldenEye*
Strand Underground Station - London Underground. Credits include: *V For Vendetta; Creep*
Tate Modern - Tate Collection. Credits include: *Children Of Men; The Constant Gardener; Match Point; Bridget Jones's Diary*
The Athenaeum - The Athenaeum Club. Credits include: *Friends & Crocodiles; Layer Cake; Wilde*
The Natural History Museum. Credits include: *Basic Instinct II*
The Palace Theatre - Really Useful Theatres. Credits include: *Match Point*
The Prospect of Whitby Pub, Wapping. Credits include: *Friends*
The Rivoli Ballroom. Credits include: *Heartlands; Spy Game*

The Royal Naval College, Greenwich. Credits include: *Amazing Grace; Hustle; Revolver; Four Weddings and a Funeral; The Madness of King George*
The United Grand Lodge of Freemasons - United Grand Lodge of England Freemasons Hall. Credits include: *Spooks; The Hitchhiker's Guide to the Galaxy; The Wings of the Dove*
The Wapping Project, Wapping - www.1st-option.com
The Windmill Theatre. Credits include: *Mrs Henderson Presents*
Tooting Bec Lido. Credits include: *Some Voices; Snatch*
Walker's Court, Soho. Credits include: *The Vice*
Waterloo Bridge. Credits include: *Alfie; Waterloo Bridge*
Westminster Underground Station - London Underground.
York House, Richmond upon Thames. Credits include: *The Wings of the Dove*

Contributors

Peter Ackroyd, Writer
Woody Allen, Director
Sir Michael Caine CBE, Actor
Gurinder Chadha, Director
Richard Curtis, Director/Writer
David Hare, Director/Writer
Christopher Hampton, Writer
Bob Hoskins, Actor/Producer
Mike Leigh, Director
Kevin Loader, Producer
Juliet McKoen, Director/Writer
John Madden, Director
Anthony Minghella, Director/Writer
JK Rowling, Writer
Christopher Smith, Director
Barnaby Thompson, Producer
Emma Thompson, Actress/Writer
Stephen Woolley, Director/Producer

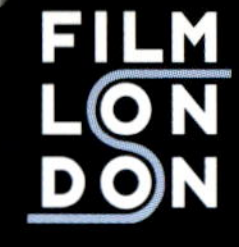

About Film London

Film London is the capital's film and media agency. Film London sustains, promotes and develops London as a major international film-making and film cultural capital. This includes all the screen industries based in London - film, television, video, commercials and interactive media. Film London is supported by the UK Film Council and the London Development Agency through Creative London. Film London also receives significant support from Arts Council England London, the European Regional Development Fund, the Mayor of London and Skillset.

Film London offers a locations service which promotes the capital as a destination for film-makers. The agency provides comprehensive information on locations, crew and the facilities available in London, as well as practical advice and on the ground support to all film-makers working in the city.

Film London wishes to thank all contributors to this project, in particular the film-makers and writers who have generously provided comments and quotes for this publication. We would like to thank the representatives of the locations who kindly gave permission for these to be photographed and included. Film London would also like to thank the London Filming Partnership and its 120 members who work to encourage and facilitate filming in the capital.

For further information about Film London please go to www.filmlondon.org.uk

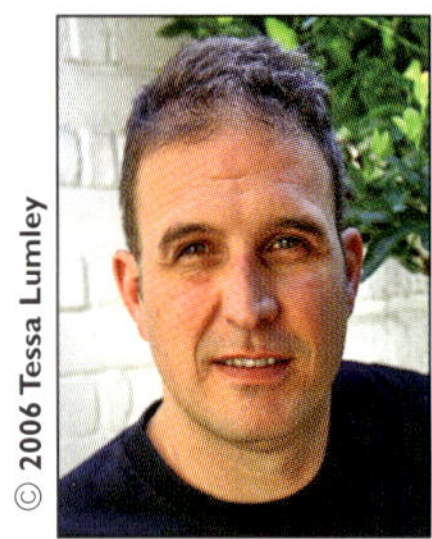

Jamie Lumley - Biography

Jamie Lumley is a professional photographer and a former Location Manager. He has worked in London, Madagascar and Borneo.

He is married with two children and lives in west London. This is his first book with Film London.

For further details of his work and current projects, please go to www.jamielumley.com